Reimagining Learning Spaces

Designing Educational Environments for a New Generation

Sue Ann Highland

CORWIN

CORWIN

For information:

Corwin
A Sage Company
2455 Teller Road
Thousand Oaks, California 91320
(800) 233-9936
www.corwin.com

Sage Publications Ltd.
1 Oliver's Yard
55 City Road
London EC1Y 1SP
United Kingdom

Sage Publications India Pvt. Ltd.
Unit No 323-333, Third Floor, F-Block
International Trade Tower Nehru Place
New Delhi 110 019
India

Sage Publications Asia-Pacific Pte. Ltd.
18 Cross Street #10-10/11/12
China Square Central
Singapore 048423

MIX
Paper | Supporting responsible forestry
FSC® C013604
www.fsc.org

Vice President and Editorial Director: Monica Eckman
Senior Acquisitions Editor: Pam Berkman
Content Development Manager: Desirée A. Bartlett
Senior Editorial Assistant: Nyle De Leon
Production Editor: Vijayakumar
Copy Editor: Tammy Giesmann
Typesetter: TNQ Tech Pvt. Ltd.
Proofreader: Gowri Kishore
Indexer: TNQ Tech Pvt. Ltd.
Cover Designer: Janet Kiesel

Printed and bound by CPI Group (UK) Ltd, Croydon, CR0 4YY

Library of Congress Cataloging-in-Publication Data

Names: Highland, Sue Ann

Title: Reimagining learning spaces : designing educational environments for a new generation / by Sue Ann Highland.

Description: Thousand Oaks, California : Corwin Press, [2026] | Includes bibliographical references and index.

Identifiers: LCCN 2025027915 | ISBN 9781071981771 paperback alk. paper | ISBN 9798348810351 adobe pdf | ISBN 9798348810344 epub | ISBN 9798348810368 epub

Subjects: LCSH: School environment | Classroom environment | Learning—Social aspects | School facilities—Design and construction

Classification: LCC LC210 .H55 2026

LC record available at https://lccn.loc.gov/2025027915

This book is printed on acid-free paper.

25 26 27 28 29 10 9 8 7 6 5 4 3 2 1

CONTENTS

Companion Website Resources

online resources

Visit the companion website at
companion.corwin.com/courses/reimagininglearningspaces
for downloadable resources.

Note From the Publisher: The authors have provided web content throughout the book that is available to you through QR (quick response) codes. To read a QR code, you must have a smartphone or tablet with a camera. We recommend that you download a QR code reader app that is made specifically for your phone or tablet brand.

DEDICATIONS AND ACKNOWLEDGMENTS

First and foremost, thank you to God for setting me on this path and filling my life with people who are truly more wonderful than I could ever put into words.

To my incredible family—thank you for always pushing me, cheering me on, and loving me unconditionally. I've got the best husband in the world—he never lets me forget who I am or what I'm capable of. And our kids? Honestly, they're the most amazing humans I know. I'm constantly in awe of the people they've become, and I can't wait to see all they'll continue to do. And now, getting to be Mimi to some pretty remarkable grandkids is an absolute joy. Thank you all for being my biggest supporters—you make my heart full.

I'm so grateful to my parents, who always encouraged me to chase my dreams and go after what I wanted. I've tried to pass that same spirit on to my children and grandchildren. That kind of belief in someone is powerful, and I hope they always feel it from me too.

To my incredible friends—many of whom feel more like family—thank you. Knowing my tribe is right there with me through all the highs and lows means everything. I couldn't do this without you.

A big thank you to School Specialty for letting me be part of a mission that truly matters—supporting students and educators. It means the world to work for a company that genuinely cares about its people and purpose. I'm thankful for the encouragement and freedom to write something that not only fits our mission but also reflects my heart for education.

And to the amazing manufacturers and industry partners—thank you for continuing to teach and support me.

Being an educator isn't just what I do—it's who I am. I feel incredibly lucky to keep doing what I love every single day.

Publisher's Acknowledgments

Corwin gratefully acknowledges the contributions of the following reviewers:

Curtis Clough
Superintendent, Corona Schools
Los Lunas, New Mexico

Ken Darvall
Principal, Tema international School
Tema, Ghana

Rich Hall
Retired Director of Elementary Education
Ashland, Virginia

Joann Hulquist
Adjunct Professor, School of Education, George Fox University
West Linn, Oregon

Neil MacNeill
Teacher, Ellenbrook Primary School
Ellenbrook, Australia

Laura Metcalfe
Education Director, Instructional Leader
Mesa, Arizona

Lena Marie Rockwood
Assistant Principal, Revere High School
Peabody, Massachusetts

Erin Schons
Assistant Director of Schools, Children's Home Society of South Dakota
Sioux Falls, South Dakota

Joan Tuttle
Independent Education Consultant
Clearfield, Utah

Richard Warren
Professor of Education, University of Maryland Eastern Shore
Princess Anne, Maryland

ABOUT THE AUTHOR

Dr. Sue Ann Highland serves as the Lead National Education Strategist for School Specialty, bringing over 30 years of experience in transforming schools and districts across the country. A retired building and district administrator, she is a recognized expert in education environments, systemic improvement, and educational change. With a master's in educational leadership and a PhD in industrial/organizational psychology, Dr. Highland specializes in developing impactful professional development programs, aligning instructional strategies with organizational effectiveness, and driving meaningful school transformation.

Throughout her career, she has held diverse leadership roles, including consultant, director of curriculum and instruction, principal, federal programs director, and career & technical education (CTE) director, with a strong focus on school turnaround and continuous improvement. She has worked extensively with public, private, and charter schools, helping them enhance instructional strategies, build leadership capacity, and create sustainable improvements.

As an industrial/organizational psychologist, Dr. Highland is passionate about aligning people, processes, and learning environments to foster success. She has provided expert coaching and consulting to districts nationwide, addressing critical areas such as crisis recovery, brain-focused instruction, collaborative learning, social-emotional learning, and career and technical education. She is particularly passionate about the intersection of instruction and environment, ensuring that physical learning spaces support and enhance student engagement and achievement.

In recent years, Dr. Highland has seamlessly integrated her extensive educational leadership experience with her work at School Specialty, designing innovative, student-centered learning environments. With a deep understanding of instructional vision and spatial design, she collaborates with districts to create dynamic, flexible learning spaces that inspire students and maximize educational outcomes.

As a nationally recognized thought leader, Dr. Highland frequently speaks at regional and national education conferences, sharing her expertise in school transformation, instructional leadership, and effective professional development. With an unwavering commitment to PK–12 school improvement, Dr. Highland partners with educators and administrators to implement evidence-based practices, streamline operations, and foster lasting success in schools and districts nationwide.

INTRODUCTION

BUILDING A BETTER FUTURE

Our current educational system simply is not meeting the needs of an increasingly diverse student population. Too many students continue to be left behind. In short, we can do better.

Often, I have found that when new instructional practices are implemented, teachers feel that what they are doing now—even though it may be yielding great results—is not good enough. This is not the case. We just want to help their instruction to make an even bigger impact. It is time to rethink our learning systems and environments to support the success of *all* students in the future. Let us design highly flexible and modern learning spaces that are more inclusive of everyone, stimulate and engage a new generation of learners, and effectively support a wide range of learning activities.

Today's children and teens face considerable challenges, and research suggests they feel quite anxious about their lives. Only a few years removed from a global pandemic, students still have not fully recovered from the trauma they experienced during this life-altering event. Meanwhile, existential crises such as climate change, gun violence, and the emergence of technologies like robotics and generative AI have created a complex and uncertain future for them to navigate.

It is no wonder, then, that anxiety and depression are at an all-time high among youth. Many students continue to feel isolated from their peers and disconnected from school—and an alarming number suffer from persistent sadness and a lack of hope.

While students must rise above tough challenges to succeed, that is also true of the educators tasked with preparing them for this complex and uncertain future. Helping students thrive will require strategies designed to address their social-emotional and academic needs. Educators must draw upon inclusive learning concepts such as trauma-informed practices and Universal Design for Learning to ensure that *all* students feel safe, welcome, engaged, and connected within the learning environment. Only by establishing this connection will students be able to flourish.

But designing an inclusive K–12 learning environment is about more than delivering fully accessible instruction or creating a classroom culture in which all students feel like part of a learning community. The design of the physical environment matters, too. How a classroom space is designed, furnished, and equipped plays a key role in whether students feel welcome in that space and how effectively they can learn. This book will help to provide a framework for creating any environment within the K–12 setting. Although this will give a global view intended for school leaders, classroom teachers can learn aspects to implement within their own classrooms.

If there is one good thing to emerge from the pandemic, it is the realization that our current educational system is failing to meet the needs of an increasingly diverse student population. Too many students continue to be left behind. In short, we can do better.

As education leaders think about how to chart a new path forward, learning space design must be a key consideration. By being intentional in our approach, we can design highly flexible and modern learning spaces that are more inclusive and welcoming for everyone, that stimulate and engage today's learners, and that effectively support a wide range of learning activities.

This book offers a roadmap for doing just that.

In **Chapter 1**, I describe the challenges facing students (and educators), using evidence to explain why our current learning environments need to change—and why standing pat is not an option.

In **Chapter 2**, I outline the critical link between the design of a learning space and the quality of instruction that occurs there, as well as student outcomes. Citing evidence, I explain how the right type of learning environment creates the conditions under which students and educators can thrive—academically, socially, physically, mentally, *and* emotionally.

Chapter 3 describes the all-important shift from classic to collaborative learning, explaining how well-designed classrooms can effectively support more active, engaging, dynamic, and student-centered learning.

Chapter 4 reveals what students need to thrive socially and emotionally—and how learning spaces can foster healthier student well-being by supporting these conditions.

Chapter 5 explains what *teachers* need to be effective, and how learning space design can meet these needs.

Synthesizing the information from the first five chapters, **Chapter 6** offers a framework for what a future-ready learning environment should include—including essential components of a modern learning environment.

Chapter 7 examines specialized learning environments such as media centers, makerspaces, and sensory rooms.

Chapter 8 explores how K–12 leaders can support a culture of continuous learning by strategically applying the six essential elements to the design of non-instructional spaces as well.

Finally, **Chapter 9** contains practical advice for how K–12 leaders can apply the lessons in this book to design future-ready learning environments in their own schools. This chapter provides a blueprint for both a pilot program and implementation of these new learning environments.

Features and Benefits

- Chapter highlights
- Illustrations of innovative student-focused learning spaces
- Tools: Self-Assessments & Worksheets
- Reflection Questions
- Key Chapter Takeaways

The message I hope to leave readers with is this: The days of a "one-size-fits-all" approach to education are long gone—and modern learning environments must be flexible and adaptable to support a wide variety of learning needs.

By reimagining learning environments for a new generation, we can create spaces that effectively support engaging, high-quality instruction using modern tools and methods. Spaces that are welcoming and inclusive of all students. Spaces where students and teachers feel safe, comfortable, and supported to do their best work. Spaces that help transition users beyond the trauma they experienced during the pandemic. Spaces that allow *everyone* to thrive.

Today's students are growing up in a world that demands more support, more flexibility, and more intentional approaches to teaching and learning than ever before—and our learning environments must evolve to meet those needs. I am calling on **school leaders, educators, communities, and policymakers** to work together in transforming schools as spaces that nurture the whole child—not just academically, but socially, emotionally, and physically.

> "Empirical evidence . . . suggests that the design of learning spaces makes a difference in student success as measured by academic engagement behavior."
> (Scott-Webber, 2014)

School leaders must lead the charge by investing in innovative spaces like wellness rooms, movement rooms, career focused rooms, and flexible classrooms that support emotional regulation, achievement, and student engagement. **Educators**, as daily witnesses to students' needs, are essential supporters in designing and using these spaces effectively—bringing their insight, expertise, and voice to the forefront of this transformation. **Communities** must step in and become a piece of the change. You must talk about what your students need, what the community needs, and step in to support change. And **policymakers** must align funding and legislation to support professional development for educators, support innovation, and understand the demands on students today-—ensuring equity and impact throughout districts across the nation.

This is more than a trend—it is a necessary shift. Let us move beyond outdated models and create schools where students are seen, supported, and empowered to succeed. Together, we can reimagine learning spaces so that they reflect the needs of today and unlock the potential of a new generation of students.

WHY OUR SPACES NEED TO CHANGE

CHAPTER 1

In this chapter, I will highlight the challenges educators face in reaching an increasingly diverse student population with a wide range of academic and social-emotional needs. I will explain how learning space design must change if we want to empower students (and teachers) for success. In later chapters, we will discover the framework for designing new learning environments.

In 2023, Lajward was an 18-year-old student living in Houston. As part of a journalism project capturing youth voices talking about the mental health crisis, Lajward said:

> *The best way I can describe being a young person today is that it's like your life is starting in a world that feels like it's ending or getting worse. Coming from a public high school that had virtually no specific resources for mental health, if I or my friends wanted help for anything from social life stress to deeper anxieties about gun violence and the climate crisis, we would have [to talk with] specific teachers that were connected to their students and genuinely supportive. However, the teachers were doing that outside of their actual jobs.*
>
> (Scalawag, 2023)

Young people today are dealing with all sorts of pressures they are not equipped to face. The college application process has become ultra-competitive, leading Lajward to compare the process of competing for a spot at a prestigious university to *The Hunger Games*. The constant presence of smartphones and social media has given rise to online bullying, while also prompting youth to compare their own lives to the impossible standards they see online.

According to one recent student health survey in Oregon, 70% of high school juniors reported feeling nervous, anxious, or on edge for several days in a 30-day period—while almost a quarter of students experienced these emotions nearly every day (Miller, 2024).

Feeling anxious, depressed, or unsafe is not conducive to learning, and the youth mental health crisis is taking a big toll on education. Chronic absenteeism has "exploded" since the pandemic, the *New York Times* reports, with an estimated 26% of public school students considered chronically absent during the 2022–23 school year—up from 15% before COVID (Mervosh & Paris, 2024).

THE CHANGING WORLD

Youth mental health is a big challenge, but it is not the only one educators face. For students to succeed academically, they need to be emotionally invested in their classes and intellectually stimulated by the material. In other words, they have to be fully *engaged* in their learning. Yet, too few students have this experience in U.S. classrooms today.

According to research, students give their school a "C+" rating in making them feel excited about learning, on average—with just 13% giving their school an "A" on this metric. While a slight majority of middle school students (54%) give their school at least a "B" in making them feel excited to learn, fewer than half of high school students (44%) do. (Gallup, 2023).

One reason for the lack of engagement is that many students do not see the relevance of their education. Students need to feel like what they are learning in class, and *how* they are learning it, will prepare them for a rapidly changing future.

The skills students will need when they graduate are not the same as a generation ago. The nature of work is now radically different: Automation and AI are replacing lower-skill jobs, and students will need more sophisticated skills that cannot be learned by simply sitting and taking in information. Developing these skills requires more active forms of learning in which students are researching, discussing, analyzing, collaborating, and creating new knowledge for themselves.

To succeed in an uncertain future, students must learn to be critical thinkers, collaborative problem solvers, creative risk-takers, and global communicators. According to LinkedIn, effective communication is the No. 1 skill that employers are looking for, and they also highly value skills such as the ability to analyze and interpret complex information, work together in teams to solve problems, and adapt quickly to changing circumstances (Brodnitz, 2024).

As the skills that students need for success are changing, technology is also changing how we learn on our own—and therefore how students expect to learn when they are at school.

The Internet has opened an entire world of information to students. Today's students are accustomed to using the web for self-directed learning at a very young age, and powerful technologies now enable them to develop, edit, publish, and share their own creative works—from blog posts and fan fiction to music, videos, and other inventions. Students are spending their free time looking up information for themselves, connecting with friends online to work on projects together, and exercising their creativity . . . and this is how they expect to learn at school as well.

According to the annual "Speak Up" survey of K–12 students from the nonprofit organization Project Tomorrow, six in 10 students in grades 6–12 say they regularly use online videos and other technology to learn about topics that interest them, beyond teacher sponsorship—and 43% engage in this type of self-directly learning at least weekly. Fifty-nine percent said they like learning when they can be in control of when and how they learn, and 48% said they wish their teachers gave them more choice in the classroom (Project Tomorrow, 2023).

"In short," Project Tomorrow said, "students want learning experiences in the classroom to replicate the types of highly engaging and purposeful learning they are doing on their own beyond the classroom."

MEETING MULTIPLE NEEDS

As educators are trying to transform instruction to make it more relevant for today's students, they are also tasked with meeting a wide range of student needs. No two students are alike, and each child learns in a different way.

Not only do students bring very different backgrounds and childhood experiences with them to school, and not only are many grappling with anxiety, depression, and various traumas that affect their ability to learn, but students also have widely varied academic needs and abilities. According to the Pew Research Center, during the 2021–22 school year, 7.3 million students—about 15% of the total public school population—were identified as having special needs. Between the 2000–01 and 2021–22 school years, all but 12 states experienced growth in their special education student populations; the biggest increase—65%—occurred in Utah. Students with autism made up 12% of those with special needs in 2021–22, compared with just 1.5% in 2000–01 (Pew Research Center, 2023). Increasingly, a majority of students with Individualized Education Programs (IEPs) are receiving at least some of their instruction within mainstream classroom environments.

Neurodiversity is also top of mind with educators today. Neurodiversity is a biological term that explains the differences in the human brain. In education, we go on to further define a neurodivergence as an umbrella term for a person who has a brain that differs from what is considered the "norm." However, we should also consider that every person faces stress, being tired, hunger, and happiness that all impact them in different ways. When we face these different states, we each may need a different kind of support. I call this neuropreference. Neuropreferences are the needs a person might experience during moments of stress, fatigue, hunger, or happiness. Think about a time when you were very tired or stressed out about a situation. This stress may push you to need a walk outside, find a quiet space, or even feel the need to dance.

The student populations that schools are teaching are also becoming more linguistically diverse. According to Navarro, English learners accounted for 10.6% of all public school students in the United States in fall 2021, up from 9.4% in fall 2011 (Najarro, 2024).

Collectively, these figures demonstrate that teachers must reach a student body with an increasingly wide range of academic and social-emotional needs. Students thrive when they have choices in the seat that fits their learning best. Figure 1.1 shows students choosing different types of floor seats.

STATUS QUO IS NOT AN OPTION

To rise to these challenges and deliver meaningful, engaging, and high-quality instruction that meets all students where they are, educators need all the help they can get.

They need positive and healthy school climates that are welcoming and inclusive of all students. They need supportive school and district leaders who listen to their concerns and provide all necessary resources. They need ongoing training and mentoring to ensure they can do their jobs effectively, with time to plan collaboratively with their colleagues. And they need counselors, school psychologists, and other professionals to make sure students are receiving the mental health support they require.

The learning environment itself is also a critical resource. As I will explain in the next chapter, how a classroom is designed, furnished, and equipped plays a key role in supporting—or hindering—both student and teacher success.

> **"Students who used flexible furniture reported greater satisfaction with the learning environment than their peers who used traditional furniture."**
>
> (Gao, et al, 2021)

A well-designed learning environment helps students feel safe, secure, comfortable, and welcome, so they can focus effectively on instruction. It helps students learn in the kinds of hands-on, collaborative ways they will need to thrive in the workplaces of the future. And it helps teachers meet a wide range of student needs and abilities.

Figure 1.1

Seating Choices Facilitate Learning

Photo Credit: Muzo Works

Yet, research from the National Center for Education Statistics (NCES) suggests that the vast majority of students are still learning in outdated school environments that are ill-equipped to meet modern requirements.

The average age of a school building in the United States is 49 years, according to an NCES survey. Nearly two in five schools—38%—were built before 1970. About a third of the nation's public schools have never undergone any major renovations, replacements, or additions (Merod, 2024).

For over a century, the traditional classroom model—characterized by neatly arranged rows of desks facing the front—was well-suited for an era when whole-class, teacher-led instruction dominated. However, the needs of students and the nature of teaching and learning have evolved significantly and change constantly. The rigid, one-size-fits-all classroom layout of the past is no longer effective in supporting the diverse, dynamic, and interactive learning experiences required today. This is no different than the one-size-fits-all instruction of the past changing to one that is more student-centered and personalized to meet students' individual needs.

Future-ready instruction emphasizes **collaboration, creativity, and hands-on engagement**, yet traditional straight-row seating **hinders student interaction, teamwork, and meaningful discussions**. In today's classrooms, students are not only reading books and taking notes but also **using technology, engaging with manipulatives, experimenting with maker materials, and programming robots**. Learning spaces must be designed to accommodate these multifaceted activities, ensuring that students can seamlessly transition between different modes of learning—whether working independently, in small groups, or as a whole class. Figure 1.2 shows a hallway hangout environment with multiple places to collaborate and work.

To truly support **future-ready instruction and learning**, classrooms must be **flexible, student-centered, and adaptable**—creating environments that foster engagement, critical thinking, and innovation. The time for rigid, front-facing rows is long gone. Instead, we must embrace learning spaces that empower students to collaborate, explore, and thrive.

The good news is, transforming K–12 learning environments does not have to be costly. Yes, new state-of-the-art spaces and furniture can help improve educational outcomes dramatically—but even minor changes can make a major difference.

Whether you are a superintendent who is building brand-new schools, a principal who is upgrading an existing building, or even a classroom teacher trying to remodel your classroom on a budget, this book will help guide you toward success.

LOOKING AHEAD

> Thoughtfully designed classrooms that promote student agency, develop collaborative spaces, and encourage hands-on learning experiences can lead to higher levels of engagement and academic success.

The challenges facing both students and educators today underscore the urgent need for converting learning environments into innovative future ready spaces. Schools that fail to evolve risk perpetuating disengagement, widening achievement gaps, and limiting students' preparedness for the complexities in today's world. However, by embracing innovative learning space design, schools can create more inclusive, flexible, and engaging environments that support diverse learning styles and social-emotional needs.

Figure 1.2

Hallway Hangout

Photo Credit: MooreCo Inc.

Investing in learning environments that foster collaboration, creativity, and well-being is not just a luxury—it is critical. Thoughtfully designed classrooms that promote student agency, develop collaborative spaces, and encourage hands-on learning experiences can lead to higher levels of engagement and academic success. Moreover, these changes can empower educators by providing them with the tools which are needed in their spaces to deliver dynamic instruction and personalized support for all students.

The future of education depends on how well schools adapt to the changing needs of students. Learning spaces must reflect the world students will enter after graduation—one that values adaptability, teamwork, and innovation. By prioritizing modern, student-centered learning spaces, educational leaders can help cultivate a generation of critical thinkers, problem-solvers, and lifelong learners.

This transformation will not happen overnight, but the need for change is clear. It will require a collective effort from educators, administrators, and communities to rethink how schools are designed. By taking action now, we can ensure that every student has access to a learning environment that nurtures their growth, ignites their curiosity, and prepares them for success in an ever-changing world.

How ready are you to implement change? Schools and districts should complete a **readiness rubric** before designing and implementing new learning environments to ensure a **strategic, informed, and sustainable** transformation. The following are several reasons why this is important prior to engaging in this journey.

Reasons to Assess Organizational Readiness

1 Assess Organizational Readiness

A readiness rubric helps schools or districts evaluate **whether stakeholders, infrastructure, and instructional practices** are prepared for change. It ensures that teachers, administrators, and the community **understand and support** the shift to new learning environments.

2 Identify Gaps and Needs

By assessing factors such as **teacher training, collaboration strategies, and instructional alignment**, a readiness rubric highlights **potential challenges** and areas that need additional support.

3 Ensure Stakeholder Buy-In

Successful implementation requires **collaboration and consensus** among teachers, administrators, and parents. Change can be met with **resistance if educators feel unprepared**. A rubric helps identify areas where the district can develop **professional development plans, clear communication strategies, and phased implementation steps** to ease the transition.

4 Measure and Sustain Success

A readiness rubric establishes **baseline data** that allows schools to track progress, measure the impact of changes, and make **continuous improvements** to learning environments over time. ●

A readiness rubric serves as a **roadmap for successful transformation**, ensuring that new learning environments are **purposeful, effective, and sustainable**. Without assessing readiness, schools risk **misalignment, wasted resources, and resistance to change**—making this an essential first step in the process. Once you have completed the Readiness Rubric at the end of this chapter, you can identify if your district or school is ready to begin the process of changing learning environments or if you should lay additional groundwork prior to these changes.

In the remaining chapters, I will describe how learning environments can adapt to meet students' academic, social, and emotional needs more effectively, leading to better outcomes. In the meantime, to identify how prepared you are to undertake this journey in your own schools, you can assess where you are with **Tool 1: Self-Assessment: How Ready Are You to Implement Change?**

Tool 1

SELF-ASSESSMENT: HOW READY ARE YOU TO IMPLEMENT CHANGE?

	READINESS FOR IMPLEMENTATION				
	FIXED MINDSET	**DEFINITION MINDSET**	**ENGAGEMENT MINDSET**	**GROWTH MINDSET**	**EMBEDDED IN CULTURE / MAINTENANCE MINDSET**
School View or Teacher Belief on: **"Learning using new environments and instructional practices in schools."**	**Optional/Not Important** Learning environments are not an important element to good teaching. While a well-designed learning environment can be beneficial, students can still learn effectively without it, and I can manage my teaching without it.	**Have To** A conducive learning environment is something our kids will need to be effective in the future, and I believe we should find ways to use these new learning environments somehow. I am not really sure on how to change my instructional practice or use this type of learning environment, but I know I probably should.	**Want To** Learning environments and instructional practices are powerful in supporting classroom learning. We have access to the best research practices that can be implemented into the classroom. We know and believe the environment can be used as a tool.	**Need To (Imperative)** Learning environments and instructional practices are *transformative*. They give us opportunities to learn and create in ways that we were not able to before. We not only have access to information, but we also create it while connecting and having conversations with other education professionals.	**Standard and Expected** Learning environments and instructional practices work with one another in an ongoing and creative way. Students understand and expect to be able to use the environment for their learning. New teachers are taught and expected to adopt these research-based practices.

(Continued)

(Continued)

Administrator involvement, support, and modelling on: **"Learning using new environments and instructional practices in schools."**	**"This doesn't apply to me"** Believes that schools have too many initiatives to support right now, and learning environments are something that can be addressed at a later time.	**"Do This"** Believes that learning environments should be implemented in meaningful ways by teachers, yet continues to facilitate professional development using the same model. Leaves the teacher responsible for designing the learning environment.	**Learning in Isolation** Is open to implementing new learning environments but may not share learning openly with others. Helps to create culture by having conversations with small groups or one-to-one conversations but may still need to share learning in a transparent manner.	**"Let's Do This Together"** Is actively engaged in their own learning and models this openly for others. Learning with open discourse is shared in one-to-one, small group, and large group settings. Creates a culture where active collaboration leads to innovation by all community members. Intentionally works towards creating a powerful culture within the school, district, and larger community.	**"Setting up the future for success"** Is not only engaged with the learning in the building, but looks both internally and externally for opportunities for staff to continue to learn. The learning culture in the building/district is non-negotiable. Learning is considered a shared experience between the learner and the teacher.
How professional development is delivered regarding: **"Learning using new**	**No Focus** There is no focus on supporting teachers in the use of the environment for learning.	**Told** Teachers are told how environments can improve learning, but no powerful examples are shown, nor do they have the opportunity	**Shown** Teachers are shown powerful examples of how environments and instructional practices can improve learning experiences for	**Experience** Teachers experience the way that environments and instructional practices can transform learning. Professional	**Shared** Professional development models what is expected in the classroom. Teachers are supported and

environments and instructional practices in schools."		to see for themselves or try new ideas.	students and promote opportunities for learning. They may get to try things on a controlled scale.	development involves teachers learning in new ways and understanding the impact environments can have on improving student learning.	motivated to take risks, explore, share, and experiment with their learning.
What it looks like in the classroom **"Learning using new environments and instructional practices in schools."**	**Innovative environments are not used and instructional Practices are static** There might be new environmental elements, but they may go unused due to insufficient professional development. They are more of a nuisance than a benefit.	**Environmental tools are seen as an "thing"** Students either use environments passively or not as an interactive tool. Only small amounts of time are relegated to the new instructional practices. Deep learning is not likely to happen because of sporadic use.	**Environments and instructional practices are shared with learners often** New environmental tools are always in the room to some extent, and students can use them and share them with others. Personal choice may be exercised but for only specific learning with the permission of the teacher.	**Environments and instructional practice are ubiquitous** Environments are similar to a pencil to each student. They are used when needed and they transform learning. Students have options for how to station themselves for different learning scenarios.	**Instructional practices guide what is needed and used within the environment** The instructional vision guides the needs of the classroom, and the adults embrace new tools as needed. The environments are flexible for future needs and uses.

Based on:Prochaska JO, Velicer WF. The Transtheoretical Model of Health Behavior Change. American Journal of Health Promotion. 1997;12(1):38-48. doi:10.4278/0890-1171-12.1.38

••• REFLECTION QUESTIONS

1. What challenges do you see in your own school or educational setting, such as youth mental health struggles and disengagement in learning?
2. How do your current learning environments support or hinder students' ability to develop critical skills such as collaboration, problem-solving, and adaptability?
3. In your assessment as an administrator, do current classroom furniture and layout support or hinder student engagement, comfort, and collaboration? What changes can be made to furniture and layout to make them more supportive?

Key Takeaways

1. **The Student Experience Has Changed**—Today's students face unprecedented challenges, including mental health struggles, social pressures, and rapidly evolving job market demands, which directly impact their engagement and academic success.
2. **Traditional Classrooms Are No Longer Enough**—Outdated learning environments do not support modern instructional methods or the diverse needs of students, making it harder for both students and teachers to succeed.
3. **Change Is Necessary and Possible**—Transforming learning spaces to be more flexible, student-centered, and technology-integrated can help bridge the gap between education and the real-world skills students need for the future.

CHAPTER 2

WHY THE LEARNING ENVIRONMENT MATTERS

In this chapter, I will describe how the design of a learning environment plays a key role in shaping what teaching and learning look like in that space, as well as how effective these activities are. Citing research, I will explain how learning space design affects factors such as student engagement, success, and well-being. The chapter concludes with a planning tool to help leaders create a strategic vision for how their learning spaces should function.

How can educators create highly engaging classroom environments that lead to deeper learning—the kind where students are so engrossed in their education, they do not want to leave when the bell rings?

There are many factors needed to produce this kind of environment. It starts with a skilled instructor and content that is directly relevant to students' lives. Teachers also need lessons that are highly motivating and activities that put students in charge of their own learning.

But the design of the learning space also matters. In fact, research shows that learning space design can have a big effect—either good *or* bad—on what instruction looks like in that space and how effective it is for students.

FACTORS FOR SUCCESS

In one of the largest studies on the topic, British researchers from the University of Salford studied 153 classrooms in 27 primary schools over the course of two research phases to identify the impact of the physical classroom features on the academic progress of the 3,766 students who were learning in those spaces. They found that classroom design was responsible for as much as 16% of the students' overall learning rates (Barrett et al., 2015).

The researchers looked at 15 design factors in particular. They discovered that seven of these had a direct effect on students' learning: light, temperature, air quality, ownership, flexibility, complexity, and color.

The first three factors relate to the naturalness of the environment and students' level of comfort there: Is there enough natural lighting? Is the room neither too hot nor too cold? Are students getting enough fresh air through a proper ventilation system?

The last two factors, complexity and color, refer to how much stimulation the room provides. Is there an appropriate level of stimulation in the space, without being overwhelming for students? Is the "color mood" suitable for the activities taking place there? Are walls painted a light color, with bright highlights or a feature wall? Are the other features in the room (such as furnishings) visually interesting and appealing?

> **"Flexible seating can therefore help to empower students and make them actors in their own learning."**
> (Vallée & Fraser, 2022)

Ownership is a measure of how connected students feel to the space. Do the distinct characteristics of the classroom allow a sense of ownership among students? Are there creative design features that make the room original? Is students' work displayed on the walls? When students feel a sense of ownership over the learning space, they are more likely to take responsibility for their learning.

Ownership also refers to the degree to which the furniture in the room is comfortable, ergonomically sound, and gives students a variety of choices in where to work—such as soft seating options, traditional desks or tables, and/or standing desks. When students are comfortable, they can focus more effectively on learning and are more likely to be productive. Having choices in where they sit and work also helps students feel more engaged and emotionally invested in their education.

Flexibility refers to whether the design of the space can effectively support various learning methods, activities, and student needs. For example, soft, comfortable seating for individual students might be perfect for independent reading, while small tables or groups of 3–5 desks arranged together are ideal for small-group collaboration.

The Salford researchers also note that to support many different kinds of activities seamlessly, classrooms should include well-defined "learning zones" that are set up in various ways. Or, they could be equipped with moveable furniture so that the teacher (and/or students) can easily change the configuration of the room to fit the task at hand (Barrett et al., 2015).

Use Tool 2.1 to brainstorm ways you might enhance these features in your own school.

Tool 2.1

FACTORS FOR SUCCESS WORKSHEET

FACTORS	ASSESS THE SPACES IN YOUR CLASSROOM OR SCHOOL	SUGGESTIONS	WHAT CHANGES MIGHT YOU MAKE TO IMPROVE UPON THESE FACTORS?
Light	Is there enough natural lighting?	Add small lamps using daylight bulbs or natural UV light lamps	
Temperature	Is the room neither too hot nor too cold?	Be sure vents are not blocked, keep chill spots away from vents or direct light to control the heat, consider using fans to circulate stale air	
Air Quality	Are students getting enough fresh air through a proper ventilation system?	Ensure dust is cleared from the room, install a room air purifier, ensure vents and windows are free of dust	

(Continued)

(Continued)

Ownership	Is students' work displayed on the walls?	Décor that reflects students' cultural diversity, display student work, don't crowd walls with too much visual "noise"	
Flexibility	Does the space support various learning methods, activities, and student needs?	Small tables, groups of 3–5 desks for collaboration, well-defined learning zones, moveable furniture	
Color	Is the "color mood" suitable for the activities taking place there?	Interesting, light colors adding plants and inspirational posters	
Comfort	Are the seating options ergonomically sound?	Soft seating options, traditional desks and tables, standing desks, creating clear pathways in areas of high congestion, reducing classroom clutter	

FOSTERING DEEPER ENGAGEMENT

Studies confirm that effective classroom design can improve student engagement and behavior.

When students feel comfortable within the learning environment, they are able to focus more intently on instruction. When their curiosity is stimulated, deeper learning and engagement can occur. Both of these conditions can be achieved much more readily within well-designed learning spaces that support student autonomy, encourage exploration, and promote a sense of safety and belonging.

Research shows that the learning environment significantly influences student engagement. A study from *Frontiers in Education* found that creating personalized educational settings, with strong teacher support, leads to higher student engagement, including higher attendance. (Ye, 2024)

To measure deeper engagement, educators can assess these primary factors:

1. **Behavioral Engagement**: Participation in academic and extracurricular activities.
2. **Emotional Engagement**: Feelings of connection to teachers, classmates, and the school.
3. **Cognitive Engagement**: Investment in learning and willingness to exert effort in understanding complex concepts.

Various methods can be utilized to measure the engagement, such as:

- **Self-Report Surveys**: Tools such as Student Engagement Instruments (SEI) allow students to reflect on their cognitive and affective engagement levels. You will find several examples of SEIs for different age groups on the University of Minnesota's "Check & Connect" page (Check & Connect, 2025).
- **Observations**: Educators monitor indicators such as time on task, frequency of student responses, and the nature of classroom interactions to gauge engagement. (Edthena, 2023)

By utilizing these assessment methods, educators can identify areas for improvement and implement strategies that foster deeper student engagement.

Studies confirm that effective classroom design can improve student engagement and behavior. In one example, a fourth-grade teacher whose inclusive classroom experienced high levels of disruptive behavior, was able to improve student engagement from less than 3% of the time to nearly 50%—just by modifying the design of the learning environment (Guardino & Fullerton, 2010).

Some of the changes this teacher made to her classroom involved creating well-defined areas for individual and group work; adding organizational elements such as shelves, hooks, and labels; creating clear pathways in areas of high congestion; and adding plants and inspirational posters. Before making these changes, the teacher reported disruptive behavior in her classroom about 90% of the time; afterward, "disruptive behavior immediately decreased," the researchers noted.

For her master's thesis, a University of San Francisco student named Giuliana Barraza reviewed numerous studies and interviewed teachers at various levels of instruction to determine the role that classroom design plays in fostering student engagement and equity. Noting that the ways in which students perceive their environment shape their overall learning experience, she wrote: "Intentional classroom design can improve student enjoyment levels and increase overall engagement."

Barraza found that by employing techniques such as reducing classroom clutter, arranging seating so that students face each other and interact with their peers, and reflecting the cultural diversity of students through decorations and other materials, educators can elicit feelings of safety, comfort, and a sense of belonging among their students. She concluded: "Teachers [can] utilize aesthetic components to excite, inspire, and motivate their students through the design of their physical learning environment" (Barraza, 2021).

Figure 2.1

Hallways Can Be Used As Expanded Learning Spaces

Photo Credit: MooreCo Inc.

SUPPORTING BETTER INSTRUCTION

A well-designed learning environment not only helps teachers engage students but also helps them deliver instruction more effectively.

Research (Rands & Gansemer-Topf, 2017) demonstrates that the design of a learning environment influences the kinds of activities that take place there. For instance, the arrangement of the physical space—and where it directs students' attention—affects how students engage with each other and with their teacher.

"The setup of your classroom space has a big impact on student learning," the University of Michigan notes. "If the physical space of the classroom can be arranged as active learning space, if it has movable chairs and tables, and students sit facing each other, this can promote interactive, collaborative, and experiential learning" (Harvey & Kenyon, 2013).

A room with rows of chairs facing the teacher's desk at the front conveys the message: *I'll talk or explain, and you listen and take notes.* On the other hand, removing the physical barriers between students and their instructor "increases instructor-student interaction and encourages an active class dynamic" (Rands & Gansemer-Topf, 2017).

Arranging desks or tables in ways that make it easy for students to work together in small groups not only supports active learning more readily—it also *encourages* this behavior among students, while making it more likely that teachers will use active learning strategies during their instruction.

In a study at the University of Minnesota, research fellow D. Christopher Brooks observed two sections of a course taught by the same instructor, with one section meeting in a traditional learning environment and the other meeting in a classroom designed specifically for active learning. He found that both the instructor and the students behaved differently, depending on the type of classroom they were in (Brooks, 2012).

The traditional classroom had rows of tables facing the front of the room, while the active learning classroom was modeled after classrooms from North Carolina State University's Student-Centered Activities for Large Enrollment Undergraduate Programs (SCALE-UP) initiative. In these classrooms, students were seated at large round tables that each held nine students, making it easy for them to break off into groups of three for collaborative work.

> **"By encouraging movement, choice, and interaction, and increasing students' sense of control, this type of classroom arrangement addresses students' physical, social, and cognitive needs."**
> (Vallée & Fraser, 2022)

Despite having lower standardized test scores, on average, the students in the active learning classroom overcame the predicted achievement gap to earn the same average grade as their peers in the traditional classroom setting. Even more significantly, how each space was arranged affected the kinds of activities that occurred there, despite the fact that the instructor tried to use the same basic teaching methods and materials.

For instance, lecturing occurred in 77% of the observational periods in the traditional classroom setting, but only 55% of the periods in the active classroom setting. Class discussions occurred in 48% more of the observational periods in the active learning classroom than in the traditional classroom.

What's more, the instructor was at the podium in the front of the traditional classroom during 95% of the observational periods, but in the active learning classroom, he was at the podium only 69% of the time. The instructor also consulted privately with students more often in the active learning classroom (55%) than in the traditional classroom (27%).

Brooks concluded: "(1) Space shapes instructor behavior and classroom activities; (2) instructor behavior and classroom activities shape on-task student behavior; therefore, (3) space shapes on-task student behavior." In particular, he noted: "Different classroom types are conducive to different outcomes" (Brooks, 2012).

ENCOURAGING STUDENT WELL-BEING

The design of a learning space does not just affect teaching strategies and student learning outcomes but also plays a key role in helping—or hindering—students' social and emotional well-being. Educators can promote better well-being by creating flexible, agile learning spaces that give students choices in where to sit, foster greater connection among students, and integrate comfort and inclusiveness into their design.

This idea is also backed by research, something I will explore more fully in Chapter 4. For instance, a team of Australian researchers (Kariippanon et al., 2018) examined eight primary and secondary schools in that country and concluded that flexible learning spaces increased students' well-being by enhancing their comfort, movement, connectedness, and inclusivity.

"Flexible learning spaces were reported to facilitate student-centered pedagogy and self-regulation, collaboration, and student autonomy and engagement," the researchers wrote. Their study defines flexible learning spaces as containing "a variety of furniture options in a relatively open space, which can be configured in various ways to facilitate a range of learning experiences and create opportunities for both individual and collaborative work."

In talking with teachers and students, the Australian researchers found that these flexible learning spaces were reportedly more enjoyable, comfortable, and inclusive, while also allowing for greater interaction between students and their peers. All of these factors contributed to better health and wellness.

The researchers concluded: "It was widely perceived that the teaching and learning taking place in [these] flexible spaces had a positive impact on the social and emotional well-being of teachers and students."

CREATING A STRATEGIC VISION FOR LEARNING SPACE DESIGN

Instructional design and learning space design go hand in hand, working together to support student success. Just as it is critical for K–12 leaders to develop a strategic vision for what instruction should look like to produce the desired learning outcomes, it is equally important to create a unified vision around learning space design.

Classrooms, common areas, media centers, and other learning spaces should be designed strategically to support the educational vision a school system has and its portrait of a graduate. The type of furniture, technology, and equipment used in these spaces plays a key role in enabling the learning strategies, activities, and culture that the district is looking to promote.

Imagine a school building filled with modern, engaging, and dynamic learning environments that encourage and support a wide variety of instructional styles and strategies, while also allowing for future evolutions in curriculum and instruction. This is the model that school systems should aim for.

Sample District Vision Statement: We will create an inclusive, student-centered learning environment that fosters engagement, equity, and innovation. We believe learning should be active, relevant, and personalized by empowering students to take ownership of their learning through hands-on, inquiry-based instruction. Our instructional approach embraces diverse backgrounds and learning styles, ensuring that every student receives the support they need through data-driven instruction, and a strong focus on social-emotional well-being.

> "Students with access to flexible seating arrangements show significantly better focus, comfort, and academic performance."
> (Sadeghi & Farahani, 2016)

To achieve this model, leaders must craft an overarching vision that defines the aesthetic and functionality of their learning spaces—in other words, what these spaces should look like and how they should operate.

Creating a single, standard model for learning space design district-wide ensures that all students have the same opportunities to learn in classrooms that are fully equipped to support the district's vision for instruction—regardless of who their teacher is or where they attend school in the district. It also ensures that every teacher has the same opportunity to teach in a classroom that is designed with success in mind.

Establishing a district-wide standard for learning space design also makes the classroom design and procurement process much simpler for everyone involved. Without formal guidelines for principals, teachers, or curriculum directors to follow, this process can be chaotic and unwieldy.

To view some existing K–12 furniture standards, use an online search engine to find the following examples:

- General Characteristics of Learning Spaces, University of Kansas
- Division 28 – Electronic Safety and Security, Jefferson County School District, August 2022
- Furniture Specifications, Santa Monica-Malibu Unified School District
- Fort Bend Independent School District, 2022 Educational Specifications

With a formal standard in place, district-level leaders can create an online catalog of furniture and equipment that fits the vision they are hoping to achieve. School leaders can choose from this catalog to equip their learning spaces in a way that maintains the character of their individual facilities, while ensuring that their choices fit within the budget and instructional design framework that the district has established.

How should K–12 leaders craft a standard for learning space design? The process begins with understanding your instructional vision and what you want teaching and learning to look like to produce the type of graduates you desire. The type of instruction you are looking to promote will shape and inform the design of your learning spaces.

The right type of learning environment creates the conditions under which students can thrive—academically, socially, physically, *and* mentally. There are many elements that contribute to a highly effective learning environment, and I will discuss these in detail in future chapters. For now, **Tool 2: School Instructional Vision Worksheet** is included here, along with a sample worksheet (Figure 2.2), as a brainstorming and planning template to help you begin to think about the vision and goals you have for your learning environments.

Figure 2.2

Sample of Tool 2.2

What is your school vision statement?

We will create an inclusive, student-centered learning environment that fosters engagement, equity, and innovation. We believe learning should be active, relevant, and personalized by empowering students to take ownership of their learning through hands-on, inquiry-based instruction. Our instructional approach embraces diverse backgrounds and learning styles, ensuring that every student receives the support they need through data-driven instruction, and a strong focus on social-emotional well-being.

What is your school instructional vision? What is the ideal student learning experience? What do you want teaching to look like? What do you want learning to look like? Feel like? What do you want to see when you walk in a classroom and throughout the building? What do you want to hear when you walk into a classroom?

Teachers are active and moving throughout the room.
Students are active, conversing with each other, making productive noise.
We want to see happy students collaborating with one another, the teacher floating as a support to students, not as just the giver of information, but a facilitator.

What teaching strategies do you want to implement at this site?

- *inquiry-based learning*
- *hands-on*

<u>SOAR analysis of the building (Strengths, Opportunities, Aspirations, and Results)</u>

S = What are the building strengths? What can you build on?

- *teachers who are excited for changes*
- *students who are already actively participating in school activities*
- *supportive families and community*

(Continued)

(Continued)

O = What opportunities do you have to improve? What do your stakeholders want?

- *want to increase attendance*
- *more opportunities for students to engage with employers*
- *more career and tech opportunities*
- *increased student engagement*

A = What are your dreams for the learning environment? What do you care deeply about?

- *flexible environments*
- *environments that mirror the work environment*

R = What results do you want? How will you know you are succeeding?

- *higher attendance*
- *higher student engagement*
- *higher graduation rate and number of students in CTE programs*

How can the learning environment help support your instructional vision and strategies? For example: flexibility, stacking, flip and nest, use in multiple spaces, height adjustable, and what types of learning areas will you be using in classes.

flexible spaces, no casters on chairs, feels like a coffee shop,
easily cleanable, spaces where students feel comfortable,
and spaces where students can take a break from their day and chill out

What is your timeline for implementation?

Fall - student, teacher, and community input sessions
Fall - initial designs and gather feedback
Spring - pilot classrooms implemented and feedback gathered
Summer - final designs
Fall 2 - order new environments
Summer 2 - installation

Tool 2.2

SCHOOL INSTRUCTIONAL VISION WORKSHEET

What is your school vision statement?

What is your school instructional vision? What is the ideal student learning experience? What do you want teaching to look like? What do you want learning to look like? Feel like? What do you want to see when you walk in a classroom and throughout the building? What do you want to hear when you walk into a classroom?

What teaching strategies do you want to implement at this site?

SOAR analysis of the building (Strengths, Opportunities, Aspirations, Results)

S = What are the building strengths? What can you build on?

(Continued)

(Continued)

O = What opportunities do you have to improve? What do your stakeholders want?

A = What are your dreams for the learning environment? What do you care deeply about?

R = What results do you want? How will you know you are succeeding?

How can the learning environment help support your instructional vision and strategies? For example: flexibility, stacking, flip and nest, use in multiple spaces, height adjustable, and what types of learning areas will you be using in classes, etc.

What is your timeline for implementation?

••• REFLECTION QUESTIONS

1. How does the physical design of a learning space impact student engagement and academic performance?
2. What are some practical ways educators can modify their learning environments to better support student well-being and active learning?
3. How can school leaders create a district-wide vision for learning space design that aligns with instructional goals?

Key Takeaways

1. Research shows that classroom design can influence student learning outcomes by as much as 16%, with factors like lighting, temperature, air quality, and flexibility playing crucial roles.
2. A well-designed learning space can foster student engagement by providing for independent and collaborative learning.
3. Schools should establish a strategic vision for their learning environments to ensure that all students have access that promotes engagement, equity, and innovation.

CHAPTER

3

FROM CLASSIC TO COLLABORATIVE LEARNING

In this chapter, I will explore the critical link between a school's instructional vision and the design of its learning spaces. I will discuss what it means to create a forward-looking vision for instruction, examining the shift from traditional models to a more collaborative, future-ready concept. I will explain how this shift is grounded in pedagogical research and what it means for learning space design in particular. The chapter ends with a guide for creating highly engaging and functional learning environments wherever you might be on the continuum from classic to collaborative learning.

Designing a school environment requires an understanding of who students are today, what skills and aptitudes they will need in the future and which instructional strategies can meaningfully impact student success.

To prepare students effectively for life after graduation, the school experience must be designed around competencies that will enable them to thrive in jobs that have not been invented yet. Hockey superstar Wayne Gretzky famously said, "I skate to where the puck is going to be, not where it has already been." School should not be about what previous generations had to know, but about what today's students need in the future.

What are the most valuable skills for the jobs of the future? The answer depends on what sources you consult, but skills such as collaborative problem solving, critical thinking, creativity, and adaptability are mentioned time and again. For instance, the World Economic Forum's *Future of Jobs Report 2023* lists the most important skills over the next five years in this order:

- Analytical thinking
- Creative thinking
- Resilience, flexibility, and agility
- Motivation and self-awareness
- Curiosity and lifelong learning
- Technological literacy
- Dependability and attention to detail
- Empathy and active listening

To guide their vision for instruction, many school districts have created what they call a "Portrait of the Graduate," which defines the essential skills that students should learn and the characteristics they should possess before graduating. Whatever process schools use to develop their own instructional vision, this activity should be collaborative and involve families and other community members. K–12 leaders should listen to what their communities want in shaping a vision that works for their particular needs.

Schools provide a broad range of services that leaders consider appropriate for their communities, and these services should align with students' needs. As designers of learning spaces, we can think of these spaces as aligning with student needs and services as well, with each space serving a specific purpose or meeting a particular need. By providing many types of spaces for both students and staff, we are better able to meet students in the moment and offer the support they need. I have included Figures 3.2 and 3.3 to illustrate the needs of students, the instructional supports schools provide, and examples of spaces that can support student needs.

Figure 3.1

A Blast From the Past

Source: iStock.com/wwing

WHAT FUTURE-READY LEARNING LOOKS LIKE

For more than a century, classrooms and other learning spaces essentially looked the same, with rows of desks facing the front of the room so that students could listen to the teacher deliver instruction (see Figure 3.1). Within the last few decades, however, this model has begun to change as learning has shifted from a passive activity to an active one and schools have moved from a classic to a collaborative form of education.

To learn the skills that will prepare them for future success, students must take ownership of the learning process. They must learn from and alongside their peers. They must understand how to find and evaluate information for themselves, think critically, innovate, solve problems, and become lifelong learners (see Figure 3.4).

As classroom instruction changes, learning environments must evolve in kind to support this transition. The shift toward active,

Figure 3.2

Continuum of Needs and Services

Continuum of Needs (list not inclusive of all needs of students and in no order)	Continuum of Services (list not inclusive of all services for students and in no order)
• Hearing • Behavior Needs • Vision • Dysgraphia • Physical Disability • 504 • Gifted Education • ADHD/ADD • Autism • Dyslexia • Physical Disability • Sensory Disorder • Depression • Anxiety • Trauma • Twice Exceptional • Intellectual Disability	• Hospital Services • General Education • RTI • MTSS • Enrichment • Self-Contained • Specialized Services • Home Services • Resource Room • Intervention • Specialized Courses • Modified Standards • Counseling • Social Work Services • Co-teaching

"Instruction is very different today. It used to be 'sit and get.' Now, there is a significantly more experiential learning. Students work in groups to solve problems with their peers, instead of working in isolation. It is more like the problem-solving you see in the real world. We need students to be able to sit individually and take a test, but also to work collaboratively and not lose valuable instructional time in making that transition. The furniture we use plays a huge role in enabling that successfully."

Matthew Widacki, Dean of Instruction, Killeen School District

collaborative, and student-centered learning environments that will meet the needs of today's learners more effectively is grounded in several bodies of research. Some of these theories include:

- Constructivism
- Social Learning Theory
- Bandura's Theory on Self-Efficacy
- John Hattie's Meta-Analysis
- Universal Design for Learning
- The Whole Child Model
- Maslow's Hierarchy of Needs

Building on the research of esteemed educational theorists, the following goals and aspirations are emphasized for their role in fostering positive student

Figure 3.3

Sample Continuum of Spaces Available for Students

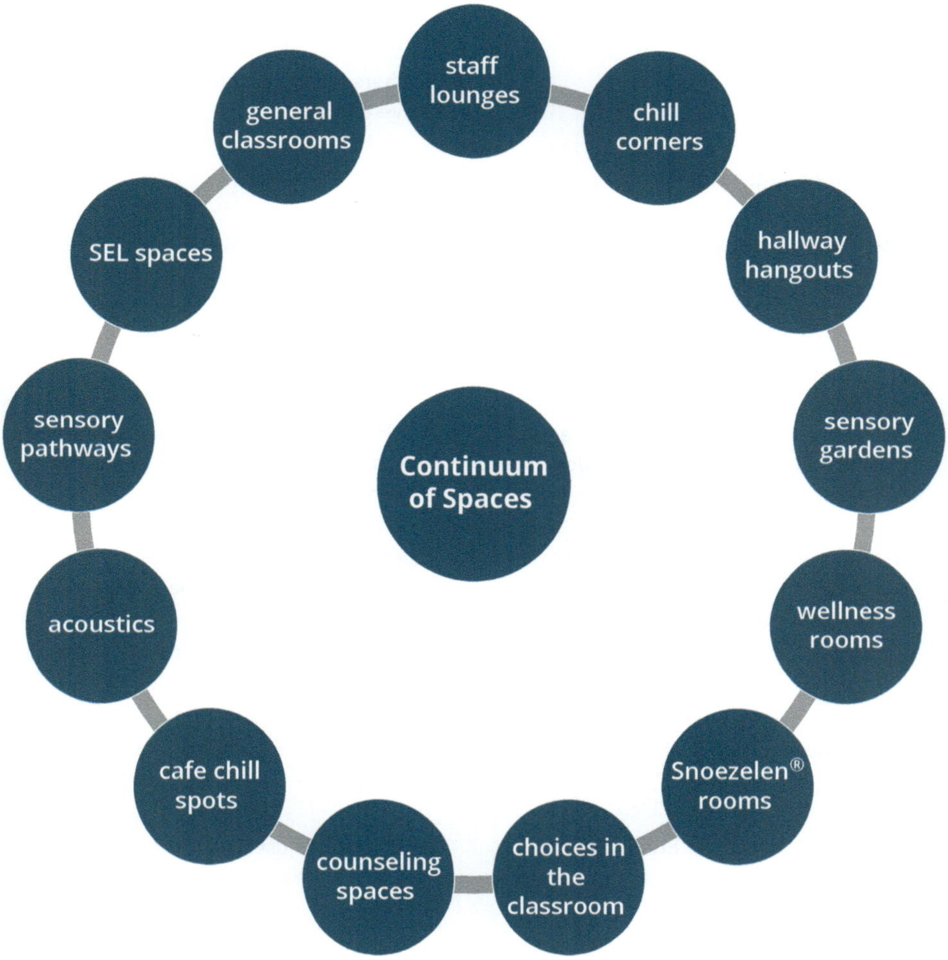

outcomes: taking ownership in their learning, learning as a social activity, achieving self-efficacy, having access to high-impact learning environments, and educators ensuring that students are ready to learn.

Student Ownership

Constructivism can be defined as learners constructing new knowledge based on what they already know. They construct

Figure 3.4

Classic vs. Future-Ready Instruction

FROM. . .CLASSIC PEDAGOGY	TO...FUTURE-READY PEDAGOGY
"A good class is a quiet class."	"Learning involves students and teachers having productive conversations."
"Keep your eyes on your own paper."	"Solve it together."
Teachers lead all instruction.	Instruction is student-led and/or student-focused.
Focused on the curriculum materials.	Focused on connecting to the real world.
The teacher "owns" a classroom and only collaborates with others during designated planning time, if at all.	Teachers share teaching spaces and have a "landing zone" that allows for ongoing collaboration.
One teacher, one lesson, one content area.	Teachers often co-teach cross-content lessons across multiple periods.
Learning is disconnected from the learner.	Learning is personal, often connected to students' areas of interest.
Little to no student agency.	Students have input into what they are learning.
Technology extremes: Either one-to-one computing or no technology integration.	Technology is used as a tool, but not full-time; instead, it is used to amplify learning.

new knowledge based on new learning experiences (Phillips, 1995). This is an active process that intends for students to take ownership of the learning process, not just serve as passive observers.

Students must be interacting with material that is in their "just right" zone. I call it the Goldilocks effect. If material is too easy, students lose interest. Too hard and they get frustrated or overwhelmed. But when material is right where it needs to be, while also stretching students a little bit, students are able to manipulate information, make inferences, and apply this learning in different contexts by themselves and with others (Vygotsky, 1978). This allows students to take agency and ownership in their learning.

Classrooms based in constructivism are typically full of discussions, interactions, and student movement. The learning environment has to be dynamic and easily adaptable, because students are engaged in more active learning. Schools can create dynamic learning environments by choosing easily moveable furniture that can be quickly arranged in various configurations to suit various kinds of tasks. Figure 3.5 illustrates how a chill spot can be a productive place for a student to sit, even during individual work time or instruction.

Figure 3.5

The Chill Spot

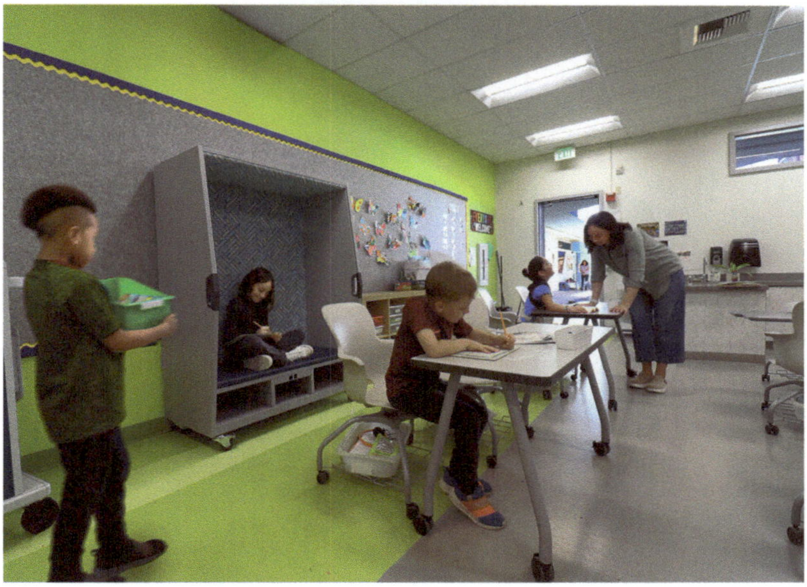

Photo Credit: Haskell Education

Learning as a Social Activity

In addition to taking ownership of learning, students working in a constructivist model also learn best by interacting with others. John Dewey, known for his theory of experiential learning, believed learning was a social activity (Dewey, 1938). By interacting with one another, students are encouraged to stay true to who they are—social beings. Bandura's Social Learning Theory builds on constructivism by asserting that people need social interaction to build knowledge (Bandura, 1986). He believes we learn through observation of others. This is critical for students because, as young children, they are highly social. As Figure 3.6 shows, people rely on individuals, the environment, and behaviors for feedback. This helps shape their behaviors.

Figure 3.6

Bandura's Social Learning Theory

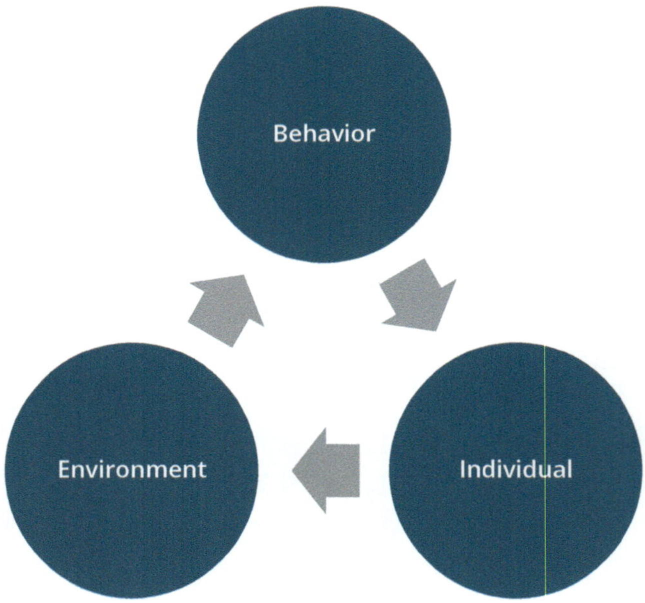

Source: Bandura (1986).

Bandura proposes five steps to learning: observation, paying attention, retention, reproduction, motivation. This aligns with the theory of gradual release of responsibility. Fisher and Frey's model (2003) states that teachers should begin with a demonstration of information (while students observe), move to supported practices, and eventually have students take ownership of the learning and demonstrate their knowledge. Bandura's Social Learning Theory believes that, by beginning with observation and moving to retention and reproduction, students are able to build motivation for learning.

Bandura further develops his theory to include self-efficacy. "Bandura (1997)0 asserts: 'Good schooling fosters psychological growth that contributes to quality of life beyond the vocational domain. The major goal of formal education should be to equip students with the intellectual tools, efficacy beliefs, and intrinsic interests to educate themselves in a variety of pursuits throughout their lifetime' (p. 214). It is apparent that growth in student autonomy is at the intersection of the learning environment and self-efficacy research and could hold some promise for transforming student perceptions of classroom environments" (Lorsbach & Jinks, 1999).

In more recent years, John Hattie's meta-analysis has given educators insight into the impact of specific teaching strategies (Hattie, 2023). According to Hattie's research, teachers have a much bigger impact on student achievement than some might think, with collective teacher efficacy having an effect size of 1.52. Again, the social aspect of education cannot be overlooked. When teachers and students are working together socially to construct and support knowledge acquisition and application, the impact cannot be dismissed.

Achieving Self-Efficacy

Self-efficacy, or the belief in one's ability to achieve a goal (Bandura, 1977), is critical for students and teachers alike. If students do not believe in themselves, they will not be able to engage with others, their environment, or the content effectively. Students must have an environment in place that supports their social-emotional needs and allows them to interact with others. By interacting socially, students can continue to build their confidence and self-efficacy.

Educators must recognize that trauma and other factors can affect a student's ability to build self-efficacy. Even if a school has future-ready learning environments, teachers who are supportive, and content that is exciting and challenging, these factors will not make a difference if students are not mentally or emotionally ready to learn.

Equity and Accessibility

As educators have become more aware of the fact that not every student learns in the same way, many have integrated the principles of Universal Design for Learning (UDL) into instruction. The UDL Framework enhances accessibility by offering multiple pathways for students to engage with content and demonstrate their learning (CAST, 2018). This approach is not limited to teaching methods but can be extended to the physical learning environment, where the design of classroom furniture plays a pivotal role in supporting diverse learning styles.

UDL can be applied to the learning environment as well. When designing physical learning spaces and classroom furniture, educators and K–12 leaders should consider a connection to the UDL principles. The following are modified from the UDL Framework:

- *Equitability*: Make the space usable by people with diverse needs and challenges. Furniture should be adaptable and accessible to students with a variety of physical and learning needs, ensuring that all students can navigate and engage with the space.
- *Flexibility*: Accommodate students' individual preferences (such as standing desks, chairs with adjustable heights, and flexible seating arrangements).
- *Simplicity*: The layout and furniture choices should be intuitive, with easy-to-use configurations that minimize distractions and enhance students' focus.
- *Perceptibility*: Classroom furniture should be designed to support all students in clearly accessing resources, whether through strategically placed seating arrangements or ergonomically designed workspaces that promote better visual and physical accessibility.
- *Low physical effort*: The space should be able to be used comfortably and efficiently. Furniture should be comfortable, easy to adjust, and allow students to move freely, reducing physical strain and promoting sustained engagement (CAST, 2018).

Ensuring That Students Are Ready to Learn

Educators are well aware that students' academic success depends on other factors, such as their emotional and physical safety and well-being—and that students cannot learn effectively if they are worried about these other factors. The Whole Child model helps us understand the definition of a successful student through a more holistic lens.

According to the ASCD Whole Child Framework (see Figure 3.7), five tenets comprise the Whole Child model: healthy, safe, engaged, supported, and challenged (ASCD, 2007). When educators help students achieve each of these characteristics at a high level, then students are poised to conquer the world. We cannot view students as merely cogs in a machine. They are human beings with their own unique challenges and circumstances.

Figure 3.7

ASCD Whole Child Framework

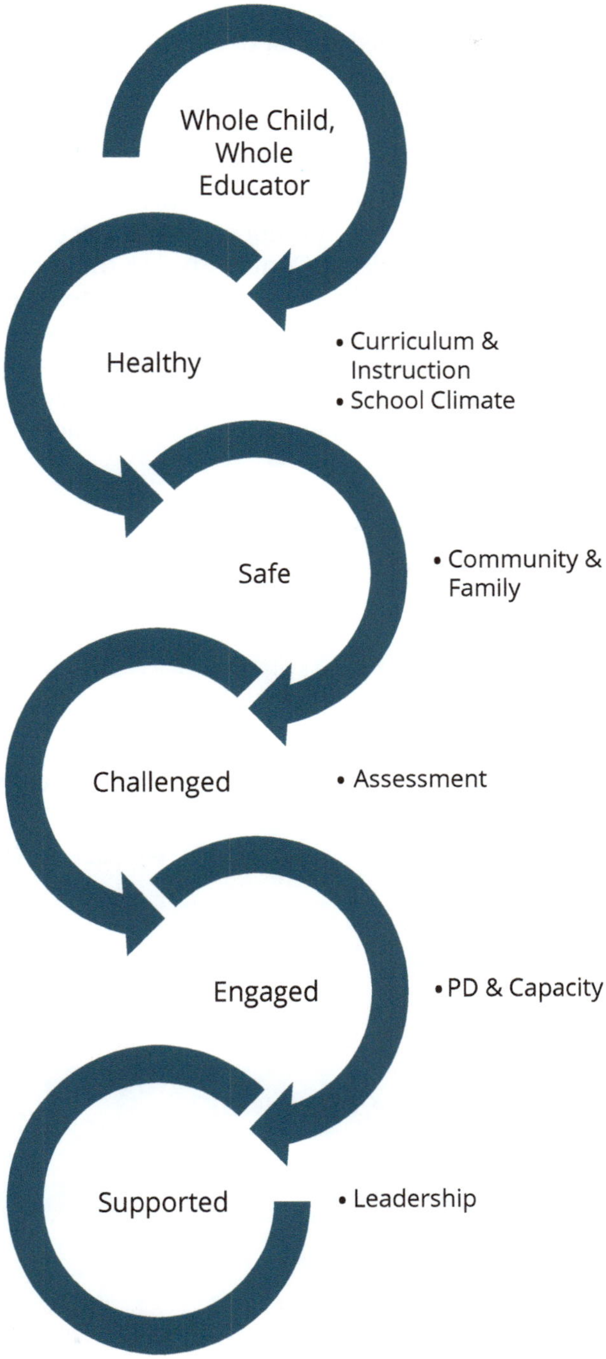

Source: ASCD (2007)

Schools can look beautiful, with modern learning environments equipped with resources to support high-quality instruction, curriculum that spirals and is personalized, and great teachers—but if a student is not healthy or well-supported, is bored, or does not have access to basic needs, then that child cannot be engaged in school.

Maslow's theory of motivation offers another way to look at students' holistic needs. First developed in 1943 and updated several times over the years, this theory has five tiers of human needs that ultimately peak in self-actualization (Maslow, 1943, 1987).

The model (see Figure 3.8) begins with physiological needs and continues with safety and security. Students (and teachers) cannot adequately function without feeling they have these basic needs in place. Continuing up the model, we move to love and belonging. This is the level where teachers shine. Creating classrooms and schools where students feel welcome, supported, and celebrated is important to supporting this level. From here, we move on to self-esteem. Only by having their basic needs met can students comfortably access higher cognitive tasks.

Figure 3.8

Maslow's Hierarchy of Needs

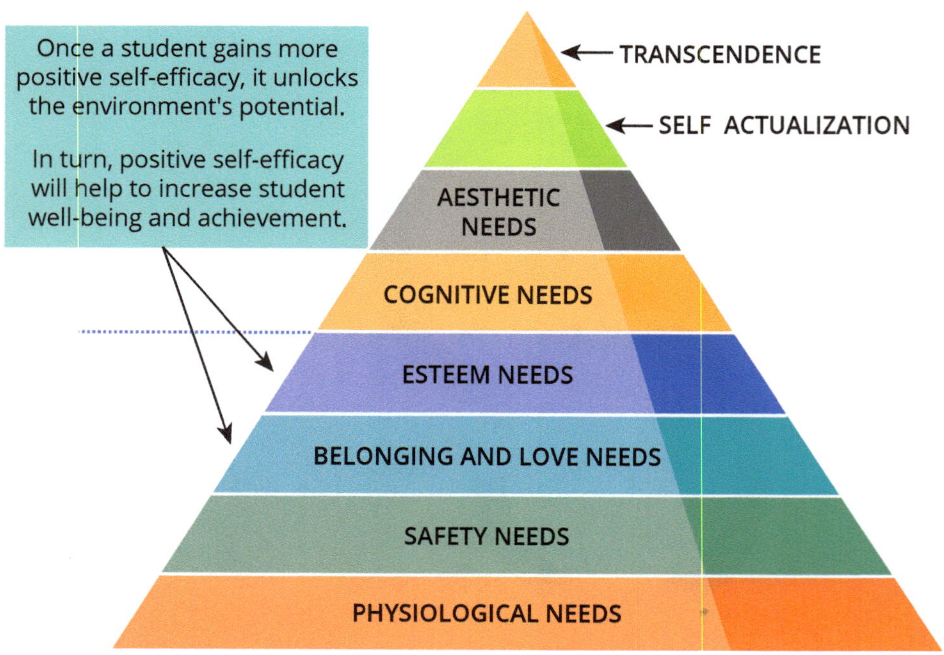

Source: Maslow (1972).

I also believe this is the point where self-efficacy kicks in for students. Only when students feel these bottom three levels have been met can they truly believe in themselves and what they can achieve. Students at this level can access higher-level cognitive tasks and make deeper connections with others.

While some people originally believed these levels were fixed, we now know they are flexible and fluid. Just like work-life balance is a myth, we know it is a myth to think that a person achieves self-actualization and then never suffers through trauma again.

If a person experiences trauma or another impactful event, they might need to reestablish those bottom levels of the pyramid. This is why people play a key role in the framework I am proposing. People matter; *teachers* matter. And we must not forget that our teachers also need this support. If teachers are worried about their own health, money, tools, and resources, they might not build their own self-efficacy. They might not be able to access higher-level cognitive tasks such as differentiating instruction or leading project-based learning.

ENVIRONMENTS TO SUPPORT MODERN LEARNING

As these theories illustrate, modern learning environments should encourage students to engage actively in the learning process. The best way to accomplish this goal is to incorporate choice and flexibility into the learning environment as much as possible.

Rather than sitting passively and listening to their teacher lecture, students are investigating, finding, and synthesizing information for themselves. Instead of repeating facts they have memorized for a test, students are demonstrating their learning by working with their peers to create new products and ideas.

Throughout all of these activities, teachers are orchestrating students' learning with a blend of whole group, small group, and individual instruction. Teachers and students are shifting frequently between these different modes, depending on which seems most appropriate for the task at hand—and this process must occur quickly and seamlessly in order to maximize learning time.

As learning becomes more active and student-centered, students need learning environments that are as dynamic as the education they are experiencing. They need learning spaces that are highly flexible and adaptable to multiple needs—spaces that *engage* and *inspire* them.

When K–12 leaders are designing learning spaces, it is important to be able to meet students where they are. In other words, make sure there are spaces that can support students' needs in multiple ways throughout the school day. And remember, one size *does not* fit all.

> **"Classrooms designed with adjustable furniture promote higher levels of participation and collaboration among students."**
> (Kepez & Üst, 2024)

There are some misconceptions that exist about the ideal type of learning environment for students. Some people believe that students should always have a fixed desk, while others say there should only be flexible seating. Neither of these extremes aptly fits a future-ready model.

To support an inquiry-based learning model, students must have the ability to choose spaces that work best for their learning. They must be able to explore their own learning, connect it to cross-curricular topics, construct their own individual meaning, and collaborate with others. Some students might prefer a more classic desk and chair combination to handle these tasks, while others might want to lay on the floor to work.

One thing distance learning taught us is that students can be autonomous with the right supports in place. Students had a taste of independence when learning from home, and they are now putting pressure on educators to allow them to learn in the ways they prefer. I would challenge anyone who says students must be in a desk and chair all day to think of how *they* worked during the pandemic. Did you always sit at a desk, or did you venture off onto the couch, your bed, or even outside? I know I did. I also watched my youngest child, who was a freshman during most of the lockdown, working during school hours. She would rarely sit at her very ergonomic desk-and-chair setup. She was on the couch, the floor, her bed, or outside—and she would even work in the hot tub sometimes while attending class online. If students are getting their work done, does it matter where they sit? And if they are more likely to focus and achieve at higher levels when they are comfortable, then does it not make sense to let them be comfortable?

Students today have lower attention spans, are technologically savvy, are aware of the world around them, and have hearts to help others (Gallup, 2023). Because of technology, they are great observers. They are also willing to challenge the status quo. Some adults might look at these qualities as negatives. Yes, these characteristics can often challenge our parenting and teaching skills, but we need to embrace the fact that these are today's students. We must recognize the positives that came out of the pandemic: an appreciation of life, the connectedness to family, and the optimism for their future. Our students are up for the challenge. We just need to provide them with learning environments that support their learning and their future work experiences.

DIFFERENT MODELS FOR VARIOUS SCENARIOS

Environments can range from classic to collaborative to future-ready. Each environment has a unique set of features that makes it function as a tool for the teacher's figurative toolkit. Figure 3.9 defines components to consider when designing school environments and Figure 3.10 compares how the considerations look in three different environments. Following Figure 3.10, you will find real examples and illustrations of the three different types of environments—classic (Figures 3.11 and 3.12), innovative (Figures 3.13 and 3.14), and future-ready (Figures 3.15 and 3.16). The computer-generated images depict environments School Specialty teams have designed and implemented in schools while the photos (Figures 3.17, 3.18, and 3.19) are completed installations from manufacturing partners.

Figure 3.9

Components to Consider in School Environments

Layout	The classroom layout is directly connected to the type of instruction delivered. Pedagogy will impact how furniture is utilized in each environment.
Furniture Movement	The furniture movement is critical to a future-ready environment because students own the setup and movement of the furniture. In a classic environment, the furniture is not typically moved, except for decoration purposes.
Seating Per Student	The type of seating in classrooms can vary. Formal seating can be described as a standard-height desk paired with a traditional chair, whereas informal seating includes alternative types of seatings such as soft seating, standing desk, or others.
Seating Assignments	In a classic environment, each student might be assigned a specific seat. A future-ready environment would allow for students to choose where they sit throughout the day or lesson. Choice is important for students to build agency for their learning.
Ratios	The ratio of formal to informal seating is determined by the needs of the instruction. A more classic environment will lean more heavily into the formal seating, where a future-ready environment will lean more towards a 50/50 split.
Mobility of Furniture	Mobility refers to the extent to which furniture is fixed or is immobile versus how much is on casters or easily moved and rearranged.
Teacher Footprint	Who owns most of the classroom real estate? The teacher footprint tends to dictate how much area the teacher desk, storage, and other items takes up within the classroom. Teachers in a future-ready environment are mobile and have a smaller footprint.
Ancillary Items	Ancillary items are additional pieces of furniture and equipment that go into the classroom. These are items such as mobile whiteboards, mobile storage, and easily accessible tools.
Additional Spaces	What additional spaces do you want to include within the classroom? Spaces to consider may include chill corners, reading corners, art centers, and computer stations.

Learning Zones	Learning zones can include spaces for student presentations, teacher-led instruction, storage, partner work, and individual learning.
6 Essential Design Elements	These are the six elements of interior design that should be considered during the actual design process and are connected to features of the actual furniture itself and how the furniture interacts with the physical environment and the people within. These will be called out in later chapters.

Figure 3.10

Learning Environment Features Comparison Chart

LEARNING ENVIRONMENT FEATURES	CLASSIC	INNOVATIVE	FUTURE-READY
Layout	Straight rows, groups of four	Multiple group sizes and configurations	Multiple group sizes and configurations, alternative seating areas
Furniture Movement	Teacher will typically move the classroom furniture around, if at all	Teacher will move the classroom furniture but will allow the students to reconfigure	Students reconfigure the classroom furniture often during instruction
Seating Per Student	Only one seat per student	Only one "formal" seat per student, additional "informal" seats	More than one seating option for each student, students may choose to sit in formal or informal seats to learn

(Continued)

(Continued)

Seating Assignment	Seating chart	Seating chart may be flexible, "home base" seating chart	Students have a choice in their seating
Ratios	100% formal seating	80–90% formal seating and 10–20% informal seating	50-50% to 80-20% formal to informal seating
Mobility of furniture	Furniture is mostly stationary	Furniture has some mobility	Furniture is mobile and flexible
Teacher Footprint	Teacher has a large footprint in the room	Teacher has a small footprint in the room	Teacher has a small footprint and is mobile during instruction
Ancillary Furniture	Ancillary furniture is used to store materials, teacher typically accesses these materials	Ancillary furniture is used to store materials that both students and teacher access	Ancillary furniture is used to store materials that both students and teacher access. Students also access and use mobile whiteboards.
Additional Spaces		Elements might include things such as: reading space and different table heights	Elements might include things such as: chill corner, reading space, maker area, and tables with different heights
Learning Zones	• Group • Teacher-led • Teacher Space • Storage	• Group • Teacher-led • Teacher Space • Storage • Partner	• Group • Teacher-led • Teacher Space • Storage • Partner • Presentation of Learning • Individual

Figure 3.11

Classic Environment Illustration A

Credit: School Specialty

Figure 3.12

Classic Environment Illustration B

Credit: School Specialty

Figure 3.13

Innovative School Environment Illustration A

Credit: School Specialty

Figure 3.14

Innovative School Environment Illustration B

Credit: School Specialty

Figure 3.15

Future-Ready Environment Illustration A

Credit: School Specialty

Figure 3.16

Future-Ready Environment Illustration B

Credit: School Specialty

Figure 3.17

High School Students Collaborating in a Future-Ready Classroom

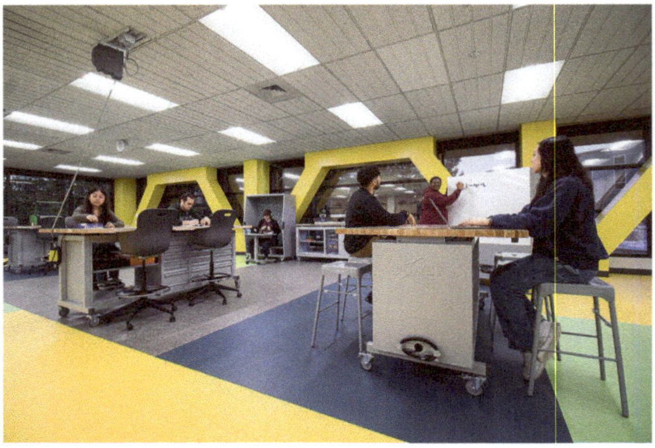

Credit: Haskell Education

Figure 3.18

A High School Renovation Reflective of an Innovative Classroom

Credit: WB Manufacturing

Figure 3.19

Preschoolers Enjoying a Lesson Integrated With Music

Credit: Muzo Works

THE SHIFT FROM CLASSIC TO COLLABORATIVE

The shift from classic to collaborative and future-ready learning is happening at different rates in each school system, and that is okay. Depending on where you are on this continuum, the design of your learning environments may look very different. You may have some elements that cross over from one type of environment to another, but this is a good place to start in creating your unique definition of what your learning environments should look like for your school or district. **Tool 3: Self-Assessment: Does the Instructional Space Foster Student-Centered Learning?** is a handy tool to help you think about where you are on this continuum—and what your ideal learning environments might look like as a result.

Tool 3

SELF-ASSESSMENT:

Does the Instructional Space Foster Student-Centered Learning?

Circle the descriptor that best describes your current classroom.

	CLASSIC	INNOVATIVE	FUTURE-READY
What is the classroom layout like? • Classic • Innovative • Future-Ready	Straight rows, groups of four	Multiple group sizes and configurations	Multiple group sizes and configurations, alternative seating areas
Who moves the furniture? • Classic • Innovative • Future-Ready	Teacher will typically move the classroom around, if at all	Teacher will typically be the one to move classroom furniture but does allow for students to reconfigure	Students reconfigure often during instruction
Do students have choices in types of seats? • Classic • Innovative • Future-Ready	Only one seat per student	Only one "formal" seat per student; there are additional "informal" seats	There is more than one seating option for each student. Students may choose to sit in formal or informal seats to learn
Do students have assigned seating? • Classic • Innovative • Future-Ready	Seating chart	Seating chart may be flexible but there is a "home base" seating chart	Students have a choice in their seating throughout the day

(Continued)

(Continued)

What is the ratio of formal to informal seating? • Classic • Innovative • Future-Ready	100% formal seating	80–90% formal seating and 10–20% informal seating	50-50% to 80-20% formal to informal seating
How mobile is the furniture? • Classic • Innovative • Future-Ready	Furniture is mostly stationary	Furniture has some mobility	Furniture is mobile and flexible
How much of the room does the teacher "own" compared to the students? • Classic • Innovative • Future-Ready	Teacher has a large footprint (ownership) in the room	Teacher has a small footprint in the room. Students have significant ownership	Teacher has a small footprint and is mobile during instruction
Who owns the ancillary furniture? • Classic • Innovative • Future-Ready	Ancillary furniture is used to store materials. Teacher typically accesses these materials	Ancillary furniture is used to store materials that both students and teacher access	Ancillary furniture is used to store materials that both students and teacher access. Students also access and use mobile whiteboards, etc
What additional spaces does the classroom offer? • Classic • Innovative • Future-Ready		Elements might include reading spaces and tables & chairs with different heights	Additional spaces might include a chill corner, reading spaces, a maker area, and tables & chairs with different heights
How many different types of learning zones are there? • Classic • Innovative • Future-Ready	• Group • Teacher-led • Teacher Space • Storage	• Group • Teacher-led • Teacher Space • Storage • Partner	• Group • Teacher-led • Teacher Space • Storage • Partner • Presentation of Learning • Individual

••• REFLECTION QUESTIONS

1. How does the shift from classic to collaborative learning impact students' ability to develop future-ready skills?
2. In what ways can educators balance structure and flexibility in designing learning environments?
3. How do theories like Constructivism, Social Learning Theory, and Universal Design for Learning shape the design of modern learning spaces?

Key Takeaways

1. **Future-ready learning environments** should be flexible, adaptable, and student-centered to support collaboration, critical thinking, and self-directed learning.
2. **Pedagogical research and learning space design** are deeply connected—constructivism, social learning, and self-efficacy theories reinforce the need for interactive and dynamic learning spaces.
3. **Equity and accessibility** in learning environments are essential to ensure that all students, regardless of background or learning needs, can fully engage and succeed in their education.

SUPPORTING STUDENTS' WELL-BEING

CHAPTER 4

In this chapter, I will describe how the design of a learning environment can also foster student well-being by promoting factors such as comfort, connectedness, and student autonomy and choice.

Educators know from experience that students cannot learn effectively if they are feeling anxious, worried, stressed out, lonely, or like they do not belong. In terms of their readiness to learn, students' mental, social, and emotional health matters just as much as their academic engagement and interest level.

This has always been true, but the pandemic underscored this point and made it impossible for anyone to ignore. Fortunately, there are many tools and resources to help educators tend to their students' social-emotional learning needs—and the design of the learning environment is one of them.

CHARACTERISTICS OF GENERATION ALPHA

Students today have very different needs than those of generations before. They face new challenges, but they are still children. Generation Alpha (the generation of people born after 2010 and before 2025) is unique, exciting, inquisitive, and very connected. They have grown up with digital devices from a very young age, and they are used to having apps and experiences that are highly customized to their needs and desires.

According to research (Springtide Research Institute, 2024), nearly all 13-year-olds say they have a smartphone, and nearly half agree they are "addicted" to it. Most spend at least a few hours on their phone daily. Though far from dominating life, feelings of loneliness crop up at least occasionally over a four-week period for four in ten 13-year-olds—and half feel worried or anxious at least sometimes during the same period.

These students need time away from their devices. They need to forge strong connections with their peers and with their teachers and/or other adults at school. And when they *do* use technology, they need to understand how to use it safely, ethically, and responsibly. They also must learn how to sift through, analyze, and synthesize the torrents of information that flood their world every day. So how do we do this? How do we help students to succeed academically, socially, and emotionally? The design of the learning environment can support these goals.

"Flexible seating is a way for the students and the teachers to learn differently.

Every child doesn't learn the same. Some of them are more comfortable in chairs. Some of them are more comfortable on the floor. And so it allows the students and the teachers to have more flexibility, not only in learning, but in teaching."

Joan Tuttle, Retired Senior Buyer, Davis School District, Utah
(Davis School District, 2020)

FACTORS CRITICAL TO STUDENTS' WELL-BEING

The U.S. Centers for Disease Control and Prevention has identified several research-based factors that are critical in helping students feel safe, supported, and connected to their school—and these feelings, in turn, improve their well-being. "School connectedness has long-lasting effects on health and well-being. Youth who feel connected at school are significantly less likely to experience health risks related to sexual health, substance abuse, violence, and mental health in adulthood" (CDC, 2024).

These factors include . . .

Comfort and security: When students are both physically comfortable and emotionally secure, they are more at ease: They can relax, block out negative thoughts, and focus more effectively on instruction.

Peer connection and support: The CDC notes: "Students who report feeling connected to, supported by, and respected by their peers show greater engagement in school. These students also report feeling more connected to their school." (CDC, 2024)

Student autonomy and empowerment: "There are positive outcomes when teachers are open to students' ideas and allow students to make choices about their learning," the CDC says.

Among these outcomes: Students are more engaged in their learning, are less disruptive in class, and feel a stronger sense of belonging and connectedness to their school.

There is a lot of overlap between the factors the CDC identifies as critical to student well-being and the six core principles from the Substance Abuse and Mental Health Services Administration (SAMHSA) for implementing trauma-informed practices within schools, childcare centers, and other public institutions.

Core Principles For Implementing Trauma-Informed Practices in Schools

1. ***Peer support***: Building connections among students and helping them feel like part of a learning community is critical in helping them overcome trauma.
2. ***Collaboration and mutuality***: Student well-being is supported by the development of healthy relationships built on mutual respect not just between students and their peers, but also between students and their teachers.
3. ***Empowerment, voice, and choice***: Healing from trauma is enhanced when students are supported in shared decision-making, choice, and goal-setting—and when they are empowered to advocate for themselves in the classroom.
4. ***Inclusivity***: Being responsive and sensitive to individual needs and differences, and helping everyone feel welcome and included, is another important factor in helping students overcome trauma and feel safe.
5. ***Comfort and Safety***: Students who are dealing with trauma need to feel both physically and psychologically safe within the learning environment. This means the space itself must be safe and secure, and the interpersonal interactions that take place there also must feel safe for students. ●

Here is a closer look at some of these principles and how the design of a learning environment can support or enhance them.

Peer Support

Building meaningful connections among students is essential for fostering resilience, overcoming trauma, and creating a sense of belonging in a learning community. Research indicates that a sense of connectedness significantly contributes to students' social-emotional well-being. Katharina Kariippanon et al. (2018) emphasized that the right learning environment can nurture this connectedness by promoting collaboration and interaction among students.

Figure 4.1

Students Can Enjoy Learning While Choosing the Seat Where They Learn Best

Source: Haskell Education

For example, learning spaces equipped with flexible, future-ready furniture that can adapt to various group sizes and activities enable students to work together seamlessly on group tasks and projects. Flexible learning environments foster stronger relationships among students, because they allow for more movement, interaction, and collaborative group work. One student in the study said, "I think I've made more friends with the group work. I know we've been in the same school for about three years, but with the group work, you become a bit closer." (Kariippanon et al., 2018)

This sense of belonging extends beyond student friendships. Collaborative environments also help students develop empathy, communication skills, and problem-solving abilities—critical competencies for academic and personal success. Teachers can further enhance peer support by designing activities that foster trust, shared responsibilities, and mutual respect within these flexible settings.

Collaboration and Mutuality

Student well-being thrives in environments where healthy relationships are cultivated—not only among peers but also between students and teachers. Positive teacher-student interactions have been linked to higher levels of engagement, motivation, and academic success. Modern learning spaces, designed with flexibility and movement in mind, play a key role in supporting these relationships.

Research teams have found that physically open and adaptable spaces, combined with active learning pedagogies, encourage more frequent and meaningful teacher-student interactions. Removing traditional classroom barriers, such as desks that are placed in one spot, allows teachers to move freely and engage with students on a more personal level. This dynamic setup helps to break down power hierarchies and creates a more mutual and inclusive atmosphere where students feel seen and supported.

Teachers in such spaces are better positioned to observe and address students' needs, whether by providing encouragement, offering guidance, or addressing challenges in real time. There is a misconception that if students are sitting in straight rows, they will be focused and on task. Students in straight rows may be distant, read ahead, fall behind, or even engage in tasks that are not connected to the content. Students who are able to interact with one another, work independently, or engage in small group work contribute to a culture of trust and mutual respect, reinforcing a positive learning experience for all participants.

Empowerment, Voice, and Choice

Creating a learning environment that supports student growth must give students a sense of agency, as students benefit greatly when they are empowered to make decisions about their learning. According to SAMHSA, this includes shared decision-making, goal setting, and the development of self-advocacy skills. One effective way to foster empowerment is by giving students choices within their learning environment.

Offering multiple seating options—such as soft seating for comfort, rocking stools for movement, or high stools at café-style tables—allows students to select what works best for their individual needs. This choice not only accommodates different neurological preferences but also fosters a sense of ownership over the learning process. When students are given choices, even with something as simple as where to sit and do their work, they become empowered and build self-efficacy.

Empowerment extends beyond seating to include the tools and materials students use. Providing diverse options for creative expression—such as digital tools, art supplies, or hands-on building materials—encourages students to take initiative and explore different methods of problem-solving. Flexible learning environments also support this differentiated instruction, allowing students to choose activities or projects that align with their interests and goals.

By granting students autonomy in these areas, schools promote responsible decision-making, build confidence, and help students feel more in control of their learning journey. Self-efficacy and empowerment are especially critical for students navigating the challenges of trauma, as they enable these students to regain a sense of stability and self-determination.

Inclusivity

Creating an inclusive and welcoming learning environment is essential for supporting all students, particularly those overcoming trauma. Flexible, modern spaces can address diverse needs and preferences, fostering equity and a sense of belonging for every learner.

Offering a variety of seating options is one way to ensure inclusivity. For instance, students with sensory sensitivities may benefit from quiet zones with soft seating, while others might prefer active areas with stools or high tables. These choices allow students to select spaces that align with their comfort and learning styles.

Sensory needs have become increasingly recognized over the last few years and should be considered throughout the learning experience to ensure inclusivity. Schools should consider how to meet these needs throughout the school day. All students, even those who may not have an identified sensory need, may have what I call "sensory preferences." We all experience times where we might need a quiet space, some movement, an opportunity to fidget, or the need to listen to some music. Think of how you studied in school or how you might work on a difficult task.

Students who have sensory needs must be able to access spaces that support these needs in many areas around the school daily. Consider creating cozy corners, multisensory rooms, hallway spots to take refuge, a quiet spot in the cafeteria, and even outdoor places that include sensory experiences. By providing these spaces and considering elements throughout the building, students can easily access what they need to help them feel safe and supported.

Flexible learning spaces promote autonomy, making it easier to accommodate students with special needs or those who identify as neurodiverse. For example, classrooms with clearly defined zones allow students to self-regulate by selecting areas that match their energy levels or emotional states, enhancing their ability to engage in learning.

These principles are backed by research. Kariippanon et al. observed that flexible learning spaces gave students more autonomy and accommodated those who had special needs. One teacher said, "I've got a child in a wheelchair. I feel that it's such a more inclusive environment for him because everyone is sitting at different levels and there's no judgment. And, he can access everything in the room, because he's not getting through rows of chairs and tables" (Kariippanon, 2018). By implementing inclusive practices through thoughtful design and intentional support, schools can create environments where all students feel safe, respected, and empowered to thrive academically and socially.

Comfort and Safety

Kariippanon et al. also found that flexible learning spaces were more comfortable and psychologically safe spaces to learn in, because they gave students choices in where to sit—including not only traditional desks and chairs but also padded chairs, beanbags, and other soft seating options. This resulted in higher levels of engagement and satisfaction with school. The researchers quoted one student as saying, "Instead of having to sit in chairs and sit up straight, we get to relax on the furniture, which is really comfortable, and so you get to learn better." (Kariippanon et al, 2018)

Fostering Autonomy and Well-Being

To foster student autonomy and emotional well-being, classroom furniture and environmental design should emphasize flexibility, comfort, and accessibility. While we will dive into more recommendations in the following chapters, this list highlights key elements that address the needs of today's learners:

- **Adjustable desks and chairs**: Allow students to choose their preferred seating style (standing, sitting, or flexible arrangements), promoting autonomy and self-regulation.
- **Cozy, quiet zones**: Incorporate soft seating options like bean bags or lounge chairs to create spaces where students can recharge, reducing stress and supporting emotional well-being.

- **Collaborative workstations**: Use movable tables and whiteboards to encourage group work, fostering collaboration and communication skills.
- **Clear, intuitive layouts**: Design spaces with minimal clutter, providing designated areas for different activities (e.g., reading corners, creative stations, or tech hubs) that allow students to take charge of their learning.
- **Natural light and calming colors**: Utilize natural light and calming color schemes to create a positive, welcoming environment that enhances emotional well-being.
- **Personalizable spaces**: Include areas where students can add personal touches to their learning environment, promoting a sense of ownership and belonging.

Figure 4.2

A Small Workspace and Presentation Area Can Be Built as an Extension to the Classroom

Source: MooreCo Inc.

GETTING STARTED

In the next chapter, I will talk about how the design of a learning environment can support *teacher* success. For now, as you think about how your learning environments can foster student wellness **Tool 4: Northstar Brainstorming Worksheet** will help you to identify your major goals, your strengths, and the milestones you want to reach. Use this with your building or district team to help you define your shared goals. This will help to lay the foundation for your vision.

Tool 4

NORTHSTAR BRAINSTORMING WORKSHEET

People & Roles – Team members and role played

Goals – What do we hope to achieve?

KPIs – How are we measuring success?

Milestones – What are the keys to this project?

Target Audience – Who are we trying to reach and why? What is important info about this audience?

Advantages & Assets – What do we have at our disposal that will help us be successful?

Hopes & Fears – What hopes do we have? What fears do we have?

••• REFLECTION QUESTIONS

1. How can flexible learning environments enhance students' sense of belonging and connectedness in the classroom?
2. In what ways does student autonomy in learning spaces contribute to their overall well-being and engagement?
3. What strategies can educators implement to balance the benefits of technology with the need for face-to-face peer interactions in the classroom? ●

Key Takeaways

1. **Comfort and Connection Matter** – A well-designed learning environment can significantly impact students' emotional well-being, fostering feelings of safety, belonging, and engagement.
2. **Student Autonomy Supports Engagement** – Providing students with choices in seating, learning methods, and collaboration opportunities empowers them and enhances their motivation.
3. **Inclusive Design Is Essential** – Learning spaces should be intentionally designed to support diverse needs, including students with sensory sensitivities, neurodiverse learners, and those experiencing trauma.

ENVIRONMENTS THAT SUPPORT TEACHERS

CHAPTER 5

In this chapter, I will examine the link between learning space and design and teacher well-being and effectiveness—and I will outline strategies for designing learning spaces and space for teacher retreats that promote teacher success. These strategies will align with the 360 philosophy you will read about in Chapter 6 for the classroom environment.

While research suggests that teachers are the single biggest factor in a student's success (Hattie, 2008), there are many things teachers need to do their jobs well. They need a positive school climate and healthy working conditions. They need an effective curriculum and support from their administration. They need high-quality, relevant, and ongoing professional development so they can reach their full potential as educators. They need appropriate tools and resources to support high-quality instruction (OECD, 2018).

The design of the learning environment is a key factor as well. A classroom that is well designed, furnished, and equipped can effectively support high-quality teaching and learning, while also leading to better student and teacher satisfaction. But a poorly designed learning environment can have the opposite effects.

Teacher satisfaction is critical, especially as attrition rates have spiked since the COVID-19 pandemic. A 2023 Chalkbeat analysis of data from 15 states showed an alarming rise in the number of teachers leaving the classroom, compared to pre-pandemic figures (Barnum, 2023). In Texas, just over 10% of the state's teachers left each year in the decade before the pandemic, and those figures were remarkably consistent. But going into the 2022–23 school year, turnover jumped to 13.4%—meaning the state lost nearly 50,000 teachers that year (Texas Education Agency, 2024). School systems can reduce or at least minimize teacher attrition by ensuring that teachers are satisfied with their learning environments (Carver-Thomas & Darling-Hammond, 2019).

TEACHER WELLNESS MATTERS

> Work-life balance is a myth (McMullen, 2022), but work-life harmony can be achieved if we put in the effort.

It is not just student wellness that is important to academic success; the mental, physical, and emotional health and well-being of teachers also matters. Teachers cannot effectively tend to their students' needs until their own needs are met.

Supporting teacher well-being is a key strategy for reducing attrition and improving teacher retention. About three out of four teachers say they are stressed, anxious, or overwhelmed (Will, 2022). K–12 leaders can minimize this stress and foster teacher wellness by creating a positive and healthy working environment for faculty.

This involves creating a school culture, policies, and practices that are responsive to what teachers need and that communicate the value of teachers to the school community. For instance, leaders should recognize employee contributions in staff meetings, newsletters, and other public venues; establish a culture of openness so that teachers can feel comfortable speaking up if they are under too much pressure; regularly review staff workloads to make sure they are achievable; and encourage self-care routines, among other measures (Hanover Research, 2021).

Work-life balance is a myth (McMullen, 2022), but work-life harmony can be achieved if we put in the effort. There is really no true work-life balance because sometimes we have family concerns or activities that take more of our time or our mental efforts. If one of my young children was sick, I know it would be difficult to concentrate on work. I knew I had to give them my time and attention. However, when it was time for parent-teacher conferences, I knew my efforts needed to be directed toward those activities. When I was a building administrator, I used to keep an eye out for my teachers who spent long days in their classrooms. I would walk around the building at the end of my day and encourage them to go home, relax, unwind, and focus on their families. I often used to joke that the candy jar in my office was actually a stress meter. I could judge the level of stress on how quickly my candy jar depleted.

As a principal, I made sure I was in classrooms, just to pop in and be present. There is so much you can see when you go into classrooms, not to observe and evaluate, but just to be there for your staff and students. You can pick up on those changes in mood and activity that might point to a greater need. Trust must be built.

The design of school spaces can also encourage teacher wellness. Teachers deserve spaces to work and relax that are comfortable and that function well. They need spaces that are designed for maximum success, equipped with tools and resources that empower teachers to thrive. They need spaces that give them opportunities to connect and collaborate with their peers.

A survey from Corgan, a global architecture and design firm, reveals how classroom design affects teachers' happiness and their effectiveness in the workplace. According to the survey, nearly all teachers said a well-designed classroom makes teaching more enjoyable (98%) and that learning space design is important to helping students learn (97%). Four out of five teachers said the design of the learning environment is important to their ability to be a good teacher, and 68% said that if they were to look for a job at another school, this would be a key factor in their decision (Marquez, 2019).

RETHINKING TEACHER LOUNGES

In many schools, teacher lounges are little more than a place to make copies and grab supplies—featuring outdated furniture and a vending machine in the corner. It is time for a change. Teachers need and deserve spaces that consider their well-being and provide them with a place of respite during a long, and often, stressful workday. When we create these spaces for teachers, they are able to connect with one another and have a sanctuary space where they feel supported. These spaces can help promote wellness, satisfaction, and retention.

Two key strategies can help to transform teacher lounges into spaces that support staff well-being—make the space comfortable and encourage human connection.

Make the Space Comfortable and Inviting

Design a comfortable and welcoming environment by including soft seating and a variety of seating options. Provide choices, such as soft chairs, couches, a quiet nook with acoustic properties, and variable height tables, so teachers can find the seat that provides them the support they need—whether they need a space to listen to music, eat lunch, chat with a colleague, or even grade a paper or two. A lounge should provide the same comfort as other industry lounge spaces (see Figure 5.1).

Figure 5.1

A Comfortable Teacher's Lounge

Credit: School Specialty

Encourage Human Connection

Teaching can feel lonely at times, because educators spend much of their day in an individual classroom attending to the needs of students rather than interacting with other adults. The design of teacher lounges should incorporate items such as tables that encourage conversation, arrangements that encourage eye-to-eye contact, and a space that feels "homey." Research, such as Emma Seppala's work at Stanford University, highlights the strong link between human connection and overall wellness. This type of space can help to foster excellent school culture and a feeling of family.

KEYS TO PROMOTING TEACHER WELLNESS AND SUCCESS

In addition to providing inviting teachers' lounges, there are five other things K–12 leaders can do to create learning environments that promote optimum teacher wellness and success.

Keys to Promoting Teacher Wellness and Success

- **Flexible, ergonomic furniture**: Adjustable desks and chairs, reducing strain from long hours of sitting or standing. Consider sit-stand desks and chairs with lumbar support to promote well-being.
- **Adequate storage solutions**: Include functional storage options (e.g., file cabinets, shelves, and locking drawers) to help teachers keep materials organized and reduce clutter.
- **Quiet, dedicated spaces for planning**: Create designated areas where teachers can focus on planning and grading without distractions. This could include acoustically sound or semi-enclosed spaces for uninterrupted work, allowing for both collaborative and solo tasks.
- **Collaborative zones**: Designate areas where teachers can work together, share ideas, and collaborate on curriculum planning. Include group workspaces or tables that support meetings and discussions.
- **Adjustable lighting and temperature controls**: Allow teachers to control the lighting and temperature in their workspace to create an environment that suits their needs. Natural light is ideal, but task lighting can be provided for added comfort and focus.
- **Comfortable break areas**: Designate comfortable break areas where teachers can relax and recharge during breaks. This could include cozy seating, coffee stations, and quiet corners for moments of respite.
- **Professional development and resource-sharing spaces**: Set aside space for professional development materials, books, and resources.
- **Visible administrative support**: Create spaces that promote easy access to administrative support, where teachers can have quick check-ins or support meetings with leaders.
- **Soundproofing and privacy**: Incorporate soundproofing materials into teacher workspaces or provide private offices for sensitive discussions, ensuring that teachers can work in a quiet, distraction-free environment.
- **Positive aesthetics and design**: Use calming colors, artwork, and decor that contribute to a positive atmosphere.
- **Maintenance and cleanliness**: Ensure that workspaces are regularly maintained and cleaned, providing teachers with a hygienic and comfortable environment to work in.

Facilitate the Balanced Use of Technology for Teaching and Learning

Supporting the balanced use of technology for instruction can help teachers be more effective. Technology can facilitate rich, student-centered learning possible. When students are equipped with a mobile device and internet access, they are empowered to learn and investigate on their own. Students can easily work alone or in groups to find and share information, create sophisticated projects, and more. Learning becomes a highly active and engaging activity instead of a passive one.

To support this vision for learning, however, students need access digital devices, as well as readily available power sources, shared interactive screens, and other resources. Teachers also need easy-to-use technology tools for facilitating instruction, such as interactive projectors, learning management systems, data analysis tools, and robust digital learning platforms. They also need professional development to ensure they can use these materials effectively, as well as timely technical support whenever they have a problem or question.

However, this should be balanced with plenty of non-screen time. Time away from the computer allows students to utilize different skills to process information. The brain engages with information differently using a pencil and paper than it does when it types on a computer. Students can process information, analyze, and synthesize through other methods such as creating posters, giving speeches, debating, or presenting information in creative ways.

Integrate Design Elements to Help Teachers Manage Behavior

Well-designed classrooms and other instructional spaces can help mitigate behavioral issues and engage students more effectively in their learning, which in turn, can boost teacher wellness and morale.

For instance, furniture and equipment that allows students to rock, stretch, and move can help them calm down, manage stress, get the "wiggles" out, and regulate their emotions. Self-soothing furniture such as fidget stools can help students effectively manage their behavior, while bubble tubes, fidget devices, and other sensory objects can help relieve stress.

Learners who find themselves overstimulated might need some time to decompress. This is why a growing number of schools are adding quiet spaces or "chill zones"—separate areas of the classroom that are available to students who need some down time.

Include Proper Lighting, Acoustics, and Ventilation

Environmental factors such as lighting, acoustics, and air quality should be at optimum levels for learning and well-being. Incorporate natural lighting wherever possible and avoid using fluorescent lights, instead choosing warmer, recessed lighting sources. If replacing bulbs or light fixtures is not feasible, light filters provide an affordable option for softening classroom lighting.

Active learning environments can be somewhat noisy. Instead of sitting in their seats and listening to the teacher talk, students are often moving around and talking with their peers. The noise this creates can make it hard for some students to focus, and it can affect teachers' health as well, such as by causing vocal strain as teachers try to make themselves heard above the din.

Sound-absorbing panels can cut down on ambient noise in classrooms and other learning environments, and sound amplification systems can help students hear instruction more effectively—while reducing the strain on teachers' vocal cords.

Proper ventilation is also essential for keeping everyone healthy and reducing the transmission of airborne viruses. Portable air purifiers and classroom air filtration systems can ensure clean, healthy air within learning environments of all sizes.

Promote Healthy Hygiene

Providing portable sinks, hand sanitizer stations, and other convenient options for students and staff to wash their hands and remove germs can encourage proper hygiene, while reducing the spread of illnesses at school.

WELL-DESIGNED SPACES SUPPORT THE ENTIRE SCHOOL COMMUNITY

Thoughtfully designed school spaces are not just a luxury—they are a commitment to teacher well-being and retention. According to the Insight Education Group, 83 percent of school systems face challenges with teacher recruitment and retention (Insight Education Group, 2020) By prioritizing the creation of well-designed spaces for educators, schools can alleviate some of these challenges, improve staff morale, and foster a more positive and productive school environment.

Supporting teacher well-being through better spaces is just one strategy in the big picture. Teacher well-being benefits the entire school community, supporting students and teachers alike. Figure 5.2 is a computer rendering of how a school might create a small lounge within a larger room. In contrast, Figure 5.3 is a computer rendering of a small space that has been converted into a comfortable lounge for teachers and staff.

Figure 5.2

A Modern Teachers' Space

Credit: School Specialty

Figure 5.3

A Teachers' Lounge in a Small Space

Credit: School Specialty

In Chapter 6, I will synthesize the information I have provided so far into a framework for designing modern learning spaces, complete with key features to consider. Take a moment now to assess your current teacher spaces by answering the questions in **Tool 5: Self-Assessment: Are We Supporting the Well-Being of Our Teachers?** It is my hope that by reflecting on these questions and discussing them with your leadership team, you will be able to turn your vision into action.

Tool 5

SELF-ASSESSMENT:

Are We Supporting the Well-Being of Our Teachers?

	PROMPTS FOR DISCUSSION AND REFLECTION	WE ARE DOING WELL ON THIS	WE NEED TO WORK ON THIS
Workload and Work-Life Harmony	Are teachers' workloads manageable, and do they have adequate time to plan, teach, and assess?		
	What have we taken off the plates of teachers so they can focus on the new requirements?		
	How are we supporting teachers in maintaining a healthy work-life harmony?		
	Are we respecting time by minimizing unnecessary meetings or administrative tasks?		
	Do we allow and encourage breaks for teachers throughout the school day and encourage them to step away from their classroom?		

(Continued)

(Continued)

Professional Development	Do we provide meaningful professional development opportunities that support teachers' growth?		
	Do we ask teachers for input and allow choice on the professional development they receive?		
Recognition and Appreciation	Do we regularly recognize and celebrate teachers' achievements, contributions, or hard work?		
	How are we ensuring that teachers feel valued and respected within our school community?		
Feedback and Relationships	Are teachers' authentic voices being heard through an effective feedback system?		
	Do teachers have opportunities to build strong relationships with colleagues and collaborate in supportive ways?		
Mental Health Support	Are we providing accessible mental health resources and support, such as counseling services or Employee Assistance Programs?		
	How are we fostering a culture that prioritizes mental health and reduces stigma around seeking help?		
Compensation and Benefits	Are salaries, benefits, and incentives competitive and reflective of teachers' contributions and efforts?		

Work Environment	Is the school environment physically and emotionally safe for teachers?		
	Are there measures in place to reduce workplace stress, such as clear policies for handling student behavior or administrative support?		
Continuous Improvement	How do we regularly assess and adjust our initiatives to improve teacher well-being?		

••• REFLECTION QUESTIONS

1. How does the design of a learning environment impact both teacher effectiveness and well-being?
2. In what ways can school leaders actively support teacher wellness to improve retention and job satisfaction?
3. How can rethinking teacher spaces, such as lounges and classrooms, contribute to a more positive and collaborative school culture?

Key Takeaways

1. A well-designed classroom and teacher space can enhance job satisfaction, reduce stress, and improve teaching effectiveness.
2. Schools can support teacher well-being by fostering a positive culture, ensuring manageable workloads, and providing spaces for rest and collaboration.
3. Simple design changes, such as better lighting, flexible seating, and improved acoustics, can create healthier and more engaging learning and working environments.

CHAPTER 6

CREATING A 360 VIEW OF THE CLASSROOM

In this chapter, I will take the information presented in the first five chapters and share a framework for describing what a future-ready learning environment should look like, including the key components it should include.

To create future-ready learning environments that encourage active and collaborative learning, facilitate high-quality instruction, *and* support students' social-emotional needs, there are several key components to reflect on. Chapter 6 will include the macro components to consider while and will dig into the micro components within the future-ready spaces. Each macro component explored in this chapter plays an important role and should be considered both individually and as a part of the bigger picture:

- Instructional vision
- People
- Safety and security
- Flexible, future-ready spaces

The School Specialty 360 Philosophy® is one that provides a framework for a district, school, or even an individual teacher to create learning spaces that support both student well-being and achievement. I developed the School Specialty 360 Philosophy to include macro components such as the ones above and micro elements within the classroom itself, which will be explored throughout. (School Specialty, 2025b). All of these elements must work in tandem to support each student's full potential.

INSTRUCTIONAL VISION

As noted in Chapter 3, the design of a high-quality learning environment begins with a school or district's instructional vision. Each learning environment should support the instructional goals that teachers and K–12 leaders have for that space. When the learning environment design and the learning goals do not align, there is friction. Just like the curriculum, the learning environment is a tool to support your instructional vision and pedagogy.

If you fill a classroom with combo desks but want to use a project-based learning (PBL) approach, there will be a disconnect between the school environment and the learning intention. Combo desks are difficult to move around, and students will have a hard time getting in and out of their seats to move around the classroom. As discussed in prior chapters, today's students need to learn using multiple modalities, and they need learning to be applicable and approachable. They need to see how the skills and content they are learning hold relevance for their lives.

For the purpose of discussion, let us continue to use PBL as our sample instructional approach. According to the Institute for Local Government, some of the components that are important to a PBL classroom are (Institute for Local Government, 2014):

- **Develop 21st century competencies:** Skills such as critical thinking and problem solving, communication and collaboration, and creativity and innovation.
- **Engage students in in-depth inquiry:** Learning is an extended process that teaches students to ask questions, use resources, and develop answers. This is not always an individual process but often done in small groups or with a partner.
- **Organize tasks around a driving question:** Students work with an open-ended question that allows them to think creatively and gets them excited to learn.
- **Encourage voice and choice:** Students make choices about the products that will be created, the process they use to work in the classroom, and how they use their time. The teacher is a guide and not always the ultimate source of information.
- **Incorporate critique and revision:** Students give and receive feedback from the teacher and one another throughout this process.

- **Include a public audience:** Students present their learning, often to an audience beyond other students in their classroom and their teacher.

In order to accomplish the instructional goals of a PBL classroom, some of the design elements to consider might include . . .

- Spaces and equipment for students to share and present their ideas in small groups or to the class as a whole, such as "huddle spaces" equipped with a shared screen or monitor.
- Flexible furnishings that allow students to easily gather in groupings of various sizes, so they can quickly ideate together in small groups.
- Maker-type spaces for students to create their final products.

Figure 6.1

Students Today Need to Move and Interact With the Content

Credit: Muzo Works

A classroom need not always include just desks and chairs, nor does it need to be 100% soft or flexible seating. Students need to own the room and control how the furniture functions. When I first began teaching, I was the one to arrange the classroom every day—and it stayed stagnant during the school day. As I began to use more of an inquiry-based approach, I allowed the students to move the classroom furnishings around, while maintaining a "home base" setup. This allowed for a quick check-in and check-out for the day, while also allowing the students to move the furniture around to meet the needs for the task at hand.

One other benefit to having classrooms that support your instructional vision is that this supports equity and access throughout the district. You would not give a different curriculum to every building in a district, so why have different learning environments? The exception to this rule is if buildings have a different instructional vision, such as a magnet school. In this case, the general education rooms should be the same, but they might have specialty areas that look different. For example, a culinary space, a media center, and a general education classroom would not have the same design. Even general lab spaces need to be designed to meet the needs in that space, such as a physics lab versus a chemistry lab. This allows for students to have the same types of learning experiences and for teachers to have the same tools available.

PEOPLE

The design of a learning environment is important, but it means nothing without well-trained teachers (and students) who understand how to take advantage of the spaces, furnishings, and equipment within that environment to support effective teaching and learning.

When considering how people will interact with each other and with the learning environment, think about ownership of the space. For example, is each teacher assigned to a specific classroom, or are teachers using shared instructional spaces? How about for planning time: Are teachers using a "touch-down" space for shared planning, discussions, and office space? Within the classroom itself, how much of the room does the teacher "own" compared to the students? I was once told that whoever owns the largest footprint of the room owns the learning. I believe this is as true as asking whose voice you hear the most when you walk into the classroom.

Also, consider the functionality of the space itself. How does the furniture work? Is it easy to operate? Can the students operate any function, such as a sit-to-stand desk? Teachers must think of the furniture in the same way we think about math manipulatives: That is, students must be taught how to use these tools.

I have often walked into a classroom with new furniture and could not find the new wobble stools that were installed—or else I would find pieces of furniture lined up along a back wall, unused. When I would ask teachers why, they often admitted that they did not know how to use a piece of furniture or said students were not using the furniture responsibly. Once we established that the students must be taught how to use the furniture properly and responsibly, things tended to go much more smoothly. Teachers must also relinquish the idea of the "quiet" classroom. Yes, there are times to be quiet—but when students are using their voices, they are digesting information, inquiring about how things fit together, and synthesizing learning.

One of the biggest components missed during a new furniture refresh is supporting teachers with professional development. I know, it seems strange to say we need professional development on a piece of furniture, but we do. When implementing a new classroom environment, be sure to provide professional learning opportunities to show teachers how to take full advantage of the new furnishings, just as you would with a new curriculum. Work with a partner on this for a two-part professional development program. The first part should include the nuts and bolts of function. How does the furniture operate? The second part should include how this new tool connects to and supports high-quality instructional practices.

SAFETY AND SECURITY

Safety and security should always be considered when planning for learning environments. This includes both the physical safety of the environment and its occupants, as well as the emotional and psychological safety of students.

Safety and Security Checklist

- Make entrances and exits fully accessible, keep walkways free of clutter, and ensure that students can easily navigate the spaces. Often classrooms can contain too much furniture. If the classrooms in your building are small, what multifunctional furniture can you place in the room so that you are not using too much space?
- Ensure full visibility into what is happening in and around the learning environment. Establish clear lines of sight within hallways, common areas, and classrooms. Avoid nooks and recesses in which someone can easily hide. Incorporate open, airy spaces into the building's design.
- Make sure the furniture you choose is ergonomically sound and age-appropriate for the students in that space, with no sharp edges or other hazards.
- Make sure any solvents, chemicals, or other potentially dangerous materials are securely stored where students cannot access them without an adult present.
- Work with an expert furniture company to ensure that the furniture you choose meets your needs. Do not be afraid to ask questions about the safety and functionality of the furniture you are choosing. ●

FLEXIBLE, FUTURE-READY SPACES

A future-ready learning space helps educators bring the school's instructional vision to life. It does this with furnishings, materials, and configurations of the space that are strategically chosen to support this vision.

For instance, if floor space is needed for certain activities, it might make sense to invest in flip and nest tables that can easily be moved to the side of the room while taking up less space. If space is at a premium, consider choosing multi-use furniture, such as storage units with writable surfaces that can double as a whiteboard for brainstorming in small groups. Furniture that can be moved around on casters can help create traffic flow in a space and are a great way to define an area of a classroom.

Formal vs. Informal Spaces

Future-ready spaces can be thought of in terms of ratios: How much formal versus informal space do you have in the classroom? A traditional desk-and-chair setup is what I would consider a formal space. This is a space for one student to have one seat. The seat is what you might consider a typical student seat—a four-leg or cantilever chair. Formal spaces include a hard writing surface where a student can do written work on their own. They might even take a formal assessment at this space.

Each student needs to be allocated a seat—whether formal or informal seat to ensure that every child is accommodated during the class period.

Learning Zones

Clearly defined learning "zones" within a classroom can help students understand where to go and what to do to accomplish various tasks, such as independent reading or small group work. You might have heard creative names for describing the various learning zones in classrooms, such as a "campfire" or "cave space." I like to use language that is straightforward, so there is no confusion as to what a space is used for. The five zones I believe must be considered when choosing furniture tools are individual, partner, small group, teacher lead, and student presentation. Figure 6.2 shows a computer-generated example of how zones can be considered in the design of a learning environment.

There may be more spaces that must be defined within a classroom, and that is completely fine. Once you establish the learning zones and define their function, then you can choose furniture to support each function. Learning zones and classroom furnishings are determined by connecting pedagogical beliefs to classroom practices.

Think about the number of students you will have working together on projects, as this could determine what type of desk or table is most suitable. If a typical group consists of four or fewer students, then some desk shapes will not support this arrangement. On the other hand, if there are five or six students in a group, another choice might be more appropriate.

Figure 6.2

Learning Zones

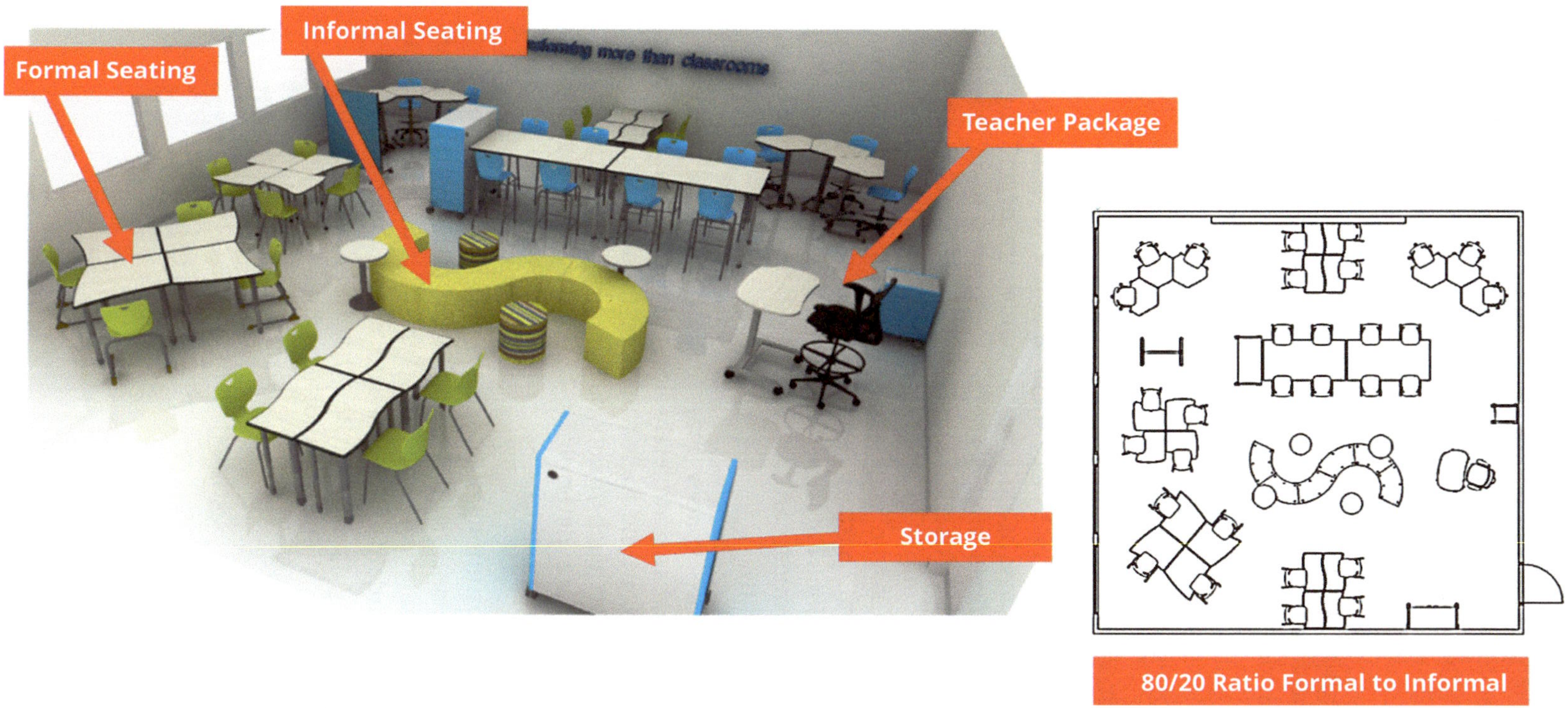

Credit: School Specialty

Questions to Consider When Furnishing Learning Zones

- Will students be working in partners or groups? If so, how often?
- How often are they moving around the room?
- When students present their learning, how will this be accomplished?
- When teachers present topics, how is the material presented?
- How much of a footprint does the teacher need for their personal items and their own workspace?
- What types of materials are being used in class, and do they require special storage?

School Specialty Six Essential Interior Design Elements®

Future-ready learning environments require dynamic spaces that are adaptable to multiple needs. Based on studies of effective learning space design, as well as what research suggests that students need for good mental, physical, and emotional health, here are six key interior design features that are critical for supporting more active and engaging learning, student wellness, and better learning outcomes (School Specialty, 2025). They are choice, comfort, versatility, connection, stimulation, and technology. These are some of the micro elements that should be considered within the future-ready spaces.

"My biggest difference is, or that I've noticed, is how more involved the kids tend to be.

Because they kind of can take ownership of where they're sitting, they're more willing to sit down and get work done. It's also a lot easier to move ourselves into groups, versus having to move desks around, which can be a lot more cumbersome. They get to collaborate. They get to work together. There is still time for a little bit of explicit teaching and then I turn it to them. And it's so much more meaningful when they are in charge of their learning. The kids love it."

Andrea Kemper, Teacher, Davis School District
(Davis School District, 2020)

1 Choice

Classrooms that include multiple seating options help students make their own choices to support how they learn best. Giving students choices in where to sit and work gets them more invested in their education. It allows them to take ownership of their learning, which leads to deeper engagement. Choice also makes classrooms more inclusive: Something as simple as having multiple seating styles to choose from can support different needs and preferences and helps students feel more welcome in the learning environment. Figure 6.3 is a computer rendering illustrating seating options within a future-ready classroom. Aside from traditional desks and chairs, consider including . . .

- Standing desks
- Soft seating options
- Ball chairs
- Rocking or swivel stools
- Café-style tables

Figure 6.3

Future-Ready Classrooms With Seating Choices

Credit: School Specialty

> "Our efforts strongly affirm the importance of providing young children with opportunities to move and to be allowed to make individual decisions about their 'place' in the classroom."
>
> (Makowski, 2017)

2 Comfort

It makes sense that students would learn best when they are comfortable. To make sure students can work comfortably, tables, desks, and chairs should be ergonomically designed and age appropriate. Because some students are sensitive to certain types of materials, learning spaces should offer seating options with different fabrics and surface types. What is more, environmental factors such as lighting, acoustics, temperature, and air quality should be at optimum levels for learning.

We know from recent research that learning space design "is pivotal for students to participate in active learning," so we want to pay special attention to student comfort (Basdogan & Morrone, 2021).

> **"When students are provided with comfortable, ergonomic furniture, they are more likely to remain focused and exhibit positive behavior."**
> (Sadeghi & Farahani, 2016)

3 Versatility

Modern learning environments must be able to support a wide range of instructional methods and learning activities. There might be times when the teacher is providing direct instruction to the entire class or to a subgroup of students, while at other times students are having a class discussion, working in small groups, or working individually. The design of the learning space should facilitate each of these activities.

One way this can be done is by using moveable, modular furniture that can be configured in different ways. For instance, students might sit at individual desks or in small groups for direct instruction and rearrange into larger groups to work on projects or into a large circle for a Socratic seminar.

Another aspect of versatility is having furniture that can serve multiple purposes simultaneously. Choosing furniture that can serve multiple purposes allows you to maximize your use of the space.

As you think about how to create flexible and versatile learning environments that can support a variety of needs, here are some elements to consider:

- Large, open, multiuse spaces
- Mobile, lightweight furniture on lockable casters
- Mobile whiteboards, AV carts, and other presentation tools
- Writeable desktop and tabletop surfaces
- Mobile storage units that easily can be modified or replaced as storage needs evolve (unlike fixed casework)
- Shelving and storage units on casters that can be used as room dividers to create smaller teaming spaces within a larger space
- Seating with built-in storage for personal belongings

- STEAM or makerspace tables with integrated storage for materials
- Corridors and outdoor spaces that can be used as extensions of the classroom

Figure 6.4

Students Can Both Lead Instruction With the Teacher and Engage With Other Students

Credit: Muzo Works

4 Connection

Education is largely a social activity, and learning spaces should be designed to support appropriate interaction between students, their teacher, and their peers.

When students discuss ideas with others, they are exposed to new perspectives they had not considered before. Working collaboratively, students can co-construct new knowledge and arrive at a deeper level of understanding than they might have on their own. Collaboration also teaches students an essential skill for success in the modern workplace. To facilitate connections between and among teachers and students see the example in Figure 6.5 and consider these design elements:

- Mobile desks and tables that can easily be arranged into flexible group sizes
- Wide, clear walkways for teachers to move around the room, listen to conversations, join a discussion, and offer support as needed
- Tools for sharing and presenting information both in person and online

Figure 6.5

Classrooms Design for Connection and Collaboration

Credit: School Specialty

5 Stimulation

Learning spaces should be designed in a way that is stimulating and engaging for students. Schools can help foster a culture of continuous learning by making both formal and informal learning spaces intellectually engaging and stimulating, with objects, artwork, and displays that encourage students to continually think, reflect, and explore. Displaying their own work gives students a feeling of ownership, which helps to increase self-efficacy.

There should be opportunities for students to move around as well: Studies show a clear connection between movement and achievement. Movement increases students' blood flow, which awakens their cells and stimulates their brains. In turn, students feel more alert and can focus more effectively on their learning.

To promote stimulation, consider design elements such as . . .

- Stools and chairs that swivel, rock, and allow for movement
- Calming objects such as soothing lights, sounds, and sights
- Opportunities for movement and activity, such as climbing, bouncing, swinging, and crawling
- Opportunities for sensory input, such as tactile sensory panels, floor tiles, and weighted blankets or other objects

6 Technology

Modern learning spaces must support a school district's vision for using technology to enhance instruction. This includes not just the technologies that will be used in the space but also the infrastructure these devices will require, such as power and connectivity.

To make sure learning spaces effectively support technology use, think about elements such as . . .

- Power supplies that are easily accessible wherever students might be working—such as mobile charging stations or built-in electrical outlets within desks, tabletop surfaces, and soft seating
- Cord management solutions that hide power cords or stow them out of the way
- "Huddle spaces" with screens and connectivity to support small group collaboration

Figure 6.6

An Example of Power Sources Integrated Into Furniture Design

Credit: Muzo works

QUESTIONS TO CONSIDER

In Chapter 7, I will look at how schools can approach the design of specialty learning environments such as media centers, makerspaces, and sensory rooms. Meanwhile, **Tool 6: What Does Your Instructional Vision Include?** is a set of questions to consider as you are choosing the furniture for your learning spaces. I have taken the top instructional strategies that both John Hattie and Robert Marzano support (Killian, 2021) and created a list of questions to consider around each strategy.

Tool 6

WHAT DOES YOUR INSTRUCTIONAL VISION INCLUDE?

HATTIE & MARZANO'S INSTRUCTIONAL STRATEGIES	QUESTIONS TO CONSIDER
Have a Clear Focus for the Lesson	How does the teacher set up the beginning of class to set the stage for the day?
Offer Overt Instruction	What options are there to set up the room for direct instruction?
Get the Students to Engage with the Content	In what ways can students engage with content in the space they feel most comfortable? What kind of choices do students have in the seating they use? What are the opportunities to learn in a less formal setting?
Give Feedback	What opportunities does the teacher have to connect with small groups throughout the class without having this space sit stagnant during most of the time? How does the teacher connect with an individual easily during the day?
Provide Students With Multiple Exposures	What are the options for students to easily reconfigure the learning environment so a teacher can present more information or give students an opportunity to do so?
Have Students Apply Their Knowledge	What spaces do students have to create their own presentation of their learning? Where can students easily access materials to work on a project?
Get Students Working Together	What are the multiple ways students can reconfigure the space to allow for shared work time? How do multiple students work together on a project with ample space? Are multiple students able to access materials at the same time?

Build Students' Self-Efficacy	How does your space allow students to connect with one another face to face? How can students use the space to get comfortable? How do students demonstrate feeling confident and in control of their learning by being able to control their space?

••• REFLECTION QUESTIONS

1. How does the alignment of a classroom's physical design with instructional vision impact student engagement and learning outcomes?
2. In what ways can educators empower students to take ownership of their learning environment, and what are the potential benefits of doing so?
3. How can schools balance safety and flexibility when designing future-ready learning spaces?

Key Takeaways

1. A well-designed classroom should support the instructional vision and allow for adaptable learning spaces that promote collaboration, inquiry, and student choice.
2. Teachers and students must be trained on how to effectively use flexible classroom furniture to maximize learning potential.
3. Safety and security are critical components of classroom design, ensuring both physical and emotional well-being while maintaining accessibility and visibility.

CHAPTER

7

MEDIA CENTERS, MAKERSPACES, MOVEMENT, WELLNESS, AND SENSORY ROOMS

In this chapter, I will take a closer look at the design considerations for specific types of learning environments, like CTE classrooms, media centers, movement, wellness, and sensory rooms.

In the previous chapters, I focused mainly on general classroom spaces. But there are other types of learning environments that have more specialized needs. Here, I will focus on spaces such as career and technical education (CTE) classrooms, makerspaces, media centers, and sensory rooms.

While features such as choice, comfort, flexibility, connection, stimulation, and technology are important to these environments as well, these specialized learning spaces also have other key design considerations that are unique to them.

CTE CLASSROOMS

CTE classrooms are becoming increasingly important to student success. Currently, more than 12.3 million students in the United States participate in CTE courses, and this number is rapidly growing (Advance CTE, 2023). CTE is no longer the old-school vocational education that many K–12 leaders grew up with. These programs prepare students for a variety of modern, highly skilled, high-paying careers, and they allow students to choose the path they want to take after high school—including college. Students can earn industry certifications that enable them to enter the workforce immediately after high school. They can also take those credits earned during high school and apply them toward a postsecondary degree. Some high school programs even allow students to graduate with an associate degree.

> **Currently, more than 12.3 million students in the United States participate in CTE courses, and this number is rapidly growing**
> (Advance CTE, 2023).

CTE gives meaning to students' education by emphasizing practical knowledge and real-world skills within a chosen career focus. It helps students understand the relevance of what they are learning in school, and it helps them set goals and focus on their future. In turn, CTE classrooms should be highly immersive learning environments that mirror the workplaces of the industries they represent.

As technology advances, the careers that students can choose after high school are changing rapidly. According to the Association for Career and Technical Education (ACTE), effective CTE programs share many characteristics: They help students learn within the context of real-world projects and scenarios. They highlight the connection between academic and technical knowledge. They incorporate modern equipment, technology, and materials regularly used within a career field. They teach not just technical skills but also important social skills needed for future success, such as creative problem solving, collaboration, and critical thinking. The learning environments for CTE programs should reflect these exciting changes.

Because career and technical skills are evolving rapidly, CTE classrooms should be designed with maximum versatility in mind, so they are easily adaptable as needs and circumstances change. For example, you might use room dividers and/or strategically placed furniture to define learning spaces in ways that can be changed as necessary without a lot of cost or effort. Movable partitions can be used to divide large, open CTE spaces into smaller rooms or spaces to fit specific needs or learning objectives. Choosing easily moveable and adaptable furniture—such as chairs that glide, furniture on casters, and modular desks and tables that quickly can be arranged into different configurations—also makes CTE learning environments highly flexible.

Be sure to consult with industry experts when designing these spaces. Just as you would ask for input from employers and professional associations when designing your CTE curriculum, you should do the same when planning the learning environment. What equipment, materials, and technologies should students be using in class to learn the skills they will need for success in that field? Look to modern workplaces for inspiration: What does a typical office, lab space, or other work environment look like in that field?

Here are some key aspects to consider when designing CTE classrooms. These factors also apply to makerspaces, innovation labs, and other hands-on learning environments that involve tinkering, prototyping, and creating:

Key Questions to Consider When Designing CTE Classrooms

- Who will be using the space?
- What tools and materials will students need to complete these activities?
- What will students and teachers be doing in the space?
- How can the environment support collaborative learning?
- What are your storage needs?
- What safety concerns does your design need to address?

Users

What are the ages and grade levels of the students who will be using the space? Understanding this will help you choose tools and materials that are safe and age appropriate, while still pertaining to the career field in question.

Equipment

High-quality CTE is characterized by active, hands-on learning, in which students complete the kinds of real-world tasks and projects they would typically encounter in that field. In the process, students learn not only important career skills but also future-ready skills that are essential in any workplace environment, such as problem solving, critical thinking, and creativity.

Based on the types of projects and activities you envision for the space, what tools and materials will students need to complete these activities? This will naturally vary by industry. For instance, an engineering CTE classroom might have mobile devices, whiteboards, and other tools for ideation; high-powered computers for running CAD software; work surfaces and materials for constructing and prototyping; and tools for students to present their ideas, such as a digital projector and/or a large-screen monitor.

Workspaces and Teaching Areas

Think about what you want students to learn and do in these learning environments, and therefore, how these spaces should be able to function. To return to the engineering example, you might have one area of the classroom where students research and brainstorm their ideas, a separate area for designing and prototyping, and perhaps a third area for presenting their ideas and sharing finished products (see Figure 7.1).

Figure 7.1

A Robotics Classroom Illustrating Flexibility in the CTE Classroom

Credit: Haskell Education

Student Collaboration

Communication and collaboration are essential skills in the modern workplace, and this is true across all career fields. Students can learn how to work effectively in teams by collaborating on CTE projects, and a well-designed CTE environment can foster and support this type of collaborative learning.

In today's office spaces, you will often see employees working together in small, impromptu groups to solve a problem. To support these types of activities, many office spaces are designed with open common areas where employees can gather in flexible groups as needed. This simple design element can easily be reproduced in a CTE learning environment. Tables and chairs that are on casters can easily be moved around the room to create fluid, agile learning spaces that support active and collaborative learning very effectively, and tables that fit together in multiple configurations can support flexible group sizes for collaborative work.

Storage

How will you safely store tools and materials when they are not in use? Make sure the furnishings you choose include plenty of storage options. Does this storage need to be built in, or can it be mobile? Mobility allows for future growth and changes that might arise in programming. Figure 7.2 shows flexibility, access, and the ability to reuse the furniture in future spaces.

Figure 7.2

Storage and Flexibility With Inclusive Seating

Credit: Haskell Education

Safety

Creating a safe working environment for students is a key consideration when designing CTE classrooms. For instance, students need plenty of space to work safely without bumping into one another. According to National Fire Protection Association fire codes, there should be at least 50 square feet per occupant in academic labs and workshops—though research suggests that a minimum of 60 square feet per student can significantly reduce the risk of accidents.

The International Technology and Engineering Educators Association (ITEEA) has issued a report with safety recommendations for CTE instruction (Love & Roy, 2022). ITEEA conducted a study of school lab facilities and found a noticeable lack of ventilation, access to eye-wash stations and showers, fully stocked first aid kits, emergency power shut-off controls, and personal protective equipment in these areas. These are all features that designers of CTE learning environments should incorporate to keep students safe.

Air filtration is another important investment schools should make when students are using 3D printers; however, this was absent in 75% of the schools surveyed. "Studies have found hazardous levels of ultrafine particles . . . are often emitted from desktop 3D printers," the report notes (Love & Roy, 2022).

Other recommendations from the ITEEA report include using a UV sanitizer to sanitize eye protection goggles after each use; installing an appropriate number of sinks with running cold and hot water sources in CTE labs and workspaces, based on class enrollment; using tape or paint to clearly designate safety work zones on the floor near all machines and equipment; and installing nonskid strips to prevent slipping and falling around any machinery (Love & Roy, 2022).

Figures 7.3 through Figure 7.9 show the various ways CTE classrooms can be designed to meet the specific needs of each classroom.

Figure 7.3

This Construction Classroom Is Ready for the Projects of Today's Learner

Credit: Wb Manufacturing

Figure 7.4

This Computer-Generated Rendering Illustrates a Modern and Immersive CTE Cosmetology Room That Feels Like a Real Salon Space

Credit: School Specialty

MODERN MEDIA CENTERS

School libraries are no longer places characterized by rows of bookcases, where students sit around blocky wooden tables and study or read quietly. Instead, they are active learning hubs that serve as a center for digital learning and teaching in many schools.

Students might be building robots or solar-powered vehicles in a makerspace section of the room. They might be recording a video in front of a green screen in another corner or collaborating with their peers to plan a business in yet another section. The media specialist might be leading a discussion on digital literacy in the center of the room, and students might be sitting at computers doing research or lounging on soft, comfortable seating throughout the library, reading or working on laptops.

Today's school library is a dynamic space that is capable of supporting a wide range of learning activities. The school library is evolving into an active learning commons where students and

Figure 7.5

This Computer Rendering Shows How a Classroom Can Integrate a "Teachable Space" Adjacent to the Lab Space

Credit: School Specialty

teachers gather to research, learn, plan, design, create, and collaborate. Figure 7.10 is a photograph of a modern library showing how the focus shifts to the students when they are provided with space to learn, read, and collaborate with others.

What does this transformation mean for the physical design of modern school media centers? As a growing share of library collections are being replaced by digital resources, media centers are using the space this frees up to support creativity, collaboration, and other rich learning experiences for users.

Today's media spaces are being used for a wide range of purposes, including student and staff research; media and digital literacy instruction; collaborative group work; makerspace activities and project-based learning; collaboration between teachers and media specialists; and more. One way to design a modern media space that can serve many purposes is to create separate zones for accommodating various types of activities.

Figure 7.6

Medical/EMT CTE Careers Are on the Rise, so We Created This Computer Rendering to Show What a Medical CTE Classroom Could Look Like

Credit: School Specialty

Figure 7.7

Veterinary Science CTE Classrooms Can Integrate Both Lab and Classroom Space as Illustrated in This Computer Rendering

Credit: School Specialty

Figure 7.8

Elementary Schools Are Implementing CTE Into Their Programs Such as This Entrepreneurship CTE Classroom Drawn With Computer Rendering

Credit: School Specialty

Figure 7.9

This Photo Shows a Flexible CTE Lab Space That Includes Tools Needed for the Program

Credit: Haskell Education

Figure 7.10

A Modern School Media Center With Many Options

Credit: MooreCo Inc.

For instance, a media center could have separate areas for researching, creating, collaborating, and presenting. Each of these zones might be equipped with furniture, tools, and materials that are appropriate for those tasks. The creating zone might include makerspace tables with built-in shelving to store materials, for instance, while the presenting zone might be equipped with an interactive whiteboard and projector.

Not every type of activity will have its own zone, as there is not enough space to create separate zones for every conceivable use of a modern media center. Therefore, designers should consider using flexible, agile furniture that can be moved around easily to create different spatial configurations—such as movable shelving and tables that can be set up in many ways.

Using fixed zones to support some activities and flexible spaces to support others will help you design a modern media center that effectively serves multiple purposes. Reflect on the questions posed in Tool 7.1 to consider some other aspects of design.

Tool 7.1

BRAINSTORMING TOOL

Activities	• What roles and purposes do you envision for your media center? Will it serve as a space for creativity and collaboration, independent reading and study, project-based learning, and teacher professional development? • How will you accommodate all these different uses? What design elements will allow you to do this effectively? How much space will be devoted to the storage and display of books and other media, and how much to programs and activities?
Culture	• How will you make your media center an open and inviting space that students and teachers will want to use? How will you attract people to the space? • What rules and norms do you want to establish for your media center? How will the design of the space reinforce those customs and behaviors?
Tools and furnishings	• What types of furniture are most appropriate to support the uses you envision? How will you balance the need for media storage and display with spaces for students to work independently and in groups? • What technology tools will be used in your media center? How will you support these tools with sufficient power and other infrastructure needs?
Seating	• What types of seating do you envision for your media center? How will you provide a variety of seating choices to support different kinds of activities, such as soft-seating options for students to cozy up with a good book, cafe-style seating for students to sit and converse, and tables for small-group collaboration?
Community use	• Will your media center be open to the community for use after school hours? How might spaces for large group instruction double as gathering places for staff, parents, or community members? • If you want your media center to be used after school hours by the community, how might you position it in a way that is easily accessible from the outside, with plenty of parking and its own separate entrance if possible?

MOVEMENT, WELLNESS, AND SENSORY SPACES

Both students and teachers need places they can relax, recharge, focus, get wiggles out, or simply take a breather. We already touched on those spaces that can support educators and staff, so let us look at these specific spaces for students. Sensory rooms are not the only places to consider. Hallways, cafeterias, media centers, and small spaces within the general education classroom are all spaces to consider. We need to meet students where they are throughout the school day to ensure they have what they need, when they need it. Consider a chill corner within the classroom that includes fidgets and comfortable seating, hallway hangouts where students can congregate or just relax and read a book.

Students may have identified needs, but they may be struggling with something on any given day. We know that, with identified needs, educators have plans in place to provide the appropriate support. Students may be experiencing trauma, divorce, being tired, hunger, or even just a run-in with another student. These sometimes-temporary situations create a need for students. Other students may have a preference to read in a quiet space, some may want to walk or move, and still others may want to be with friends. These preferences are ones I call neuro-preferences. I know when I study, I love music or noise to be in the background while my husband prefers a quiet space. I prefer to cuddle up with a good pillow and blanket, while my husband prefers to be at his desk. I am what my husband calls a wanderer when I work. You might find me at my desk in the office, on a mobile sit-to-stand desk moving around the house, or even outside on a beautiful day. When the pandemic caused students to move online, my daughter certainly did not sit at her desk every day. She would lay on her bed, sit on the floor, move to the couch, and even sit in the hot tub to listen to her online classes. She was autonomous in her choices because that was the way she wanted to learn.

Movement Spaces

Because of these various needs, we should consider additional spaces that help support sensory needs, movement, and wellness. Movement rooms in K–12 schools are gaining strong support from educators, parents, and healthcare professionals because of their positive impact on student development and learning. These rooms provide a controlled environment where students can engage in physical activity that supports self-regulation, improves focus, and enhances emotional well-being. Especially for students with ADHD, autism, sensory processing challenges, or anxiety, movement rooms offer a proactive approach to managing behaviors and emotions in a safe, structured way. Rather than punishing students for excess energy or dysregulation, schools are beginning to recognize the value of movement as a tool for helping students reset and return to the classroom ready to learn. These rooms should not be considered a punishment or reward, but simply part of the overall educational program.

When designing a movement room, several key components should be considered. First, a variety of equipment should be included to support different types of movement and sensory input—such as swings, climbing walls, crash pads, balance beams, resistance bands, tunnels, and textured mats. These tools help students develop motor coordination, core strength, and spatial awareness, while also providing calming or alerting sensory experiences. Second, safety must be prioritized through padded flooring, secure anchoring for equipment, and clear supervision guidelines. Third, the space should be flexible and adaptable to meet the needs of a wide range of students, including those with mobility issues or different sensory preferences. It is also important to create zones within the room—for example, active zones for jumping and climbing, and quiet zones for deep pressure or relaxation activities like weighted blankets or dim lighting.

To ensure effectiveness, collaboration with occupational therapists, special education staff, and mental health professionals is essential. Their input can guide both the design and daily use of the room, helping to create protocols for when and how students access the space. Overall, movement rooms reflect a growing understanding in education that physical movement is not a distraction from learning—but a powerful support for it.

Wellness Spaces

Wellness spaces in K–12 schools are becoming a powerful and necessary resource as schools recognize the connection between mental health and academic success. With anxiety, depression, and emotional dysregulation among students, these dedicated spaces provide a supportive environment where students can pause, reset, and healthily develop coping skills. Unlike clinical or disciplinary spaces, wellness rooms offer a warm, welcoming atmosphere designed to reduce stigma around mental health and create a culture of support and care. They offer a restorative approach, giving students a chance to de-escalate, practice self-regulation, and return to learning with renewed focus.

The design and function of a wellness room are key to its effectiveness. These spaces should include a mix of calming elements: soft lighting, neutral or nature-inspired colors, comfortable seating like bean bags or floor cushions, and acoustic noise-reducing materials to maintain a peaceful environment. Tools for emotional regulation—such as breathing cards, journaling prompts, sensory bins, fidget tools, and weighted blankets—offer students opportunities to explore different strategies for managing stress. These rooms can be used in all grades from kindergarten to twelfth grade. The spaces should be adapted for different age groups and needs, with clear usage protocols that allow for both scheduled visits and as-needed check-ins.

For school counselors and psychologists, wellness rooms signal a shift in how mental health services are delivered in schools. Rather than being confined to a traditional office setting with a referral-based model, counselors can use wellness rooms as a hub for visibility, approachability, and proactive student support. Office space can often be adjacent to these rooms or included in the space itself. Privacy should be considered when preparing the space. It reimagines the counselor's role—not just as a crisis responder or academic advisor, but as a champion for emotional well-being, resilience, and school-wide mental health initiatives. The room becomes a place where students can build positive relationships with others or concentrate on themselves. By integrating wellness rooms into the fabric of the school day, educators and counselors send a powerful message: every student deserves a safe space to feel seen, supported, and inspired. Figure 7.11 is a computer-generated rendering showing how a small space can become a powerful tool for teachers in this chill space.

Figure 7.11

Chill Corner

Credit: School Specialty

Figure 7.12

Hallway Spaces Can Help Students to Relax, Hang Out, Read a Book, or Even Work on Schoolwork

Credit: School Specialty

Multi-Sensory Environments

In a growing number of schools, sensory spaces have become an important element of learning space design. There is a good reason for this trend: These spaces have proven effective in helping students with anxiety or sensory processing challenges to relax, making them better able to focus and engage in learning.

Some children, such as those on the autism spectrum, can easily become overwhelmed by the sights, sounds, and other sensory inputs within their environment. A calming sensory room gives them a place to go where they can regulate their emotions before returning to the classroom.

But sensory spaces are not just for special-needs students. Anxiety is something that affects students of all ages and abilities, and the COVID-19 pandemic only amplified this challenge. A sensory room can help any student who is feeling anxious or stressed out to calm down and become more receptive to instruction.

Students cannot learn well if they are anxious, overstimulated, upset, or otherwise distracted. A sensory room can help them regulate their emotions, so they can focus more effectively on instruction. In one study, researchers found that students in Muskegon County, Michigan, were 56% more engaged in classroom activities after using a sensory room (Spyhalski, 2019).

Sensory rooms help schools meet UDL goals referenced in earlier chapters to create more inclusive learning environments for everyone. These rooms often include gentle lighting and soothing sounds, along with furniture that helps define spatial boundaries to help children feel secure in their physical space and other sensory tools that help promote self-regulation. Here are some common elements of calming sensory rooms:

- Soothing lights, sounds, and sights
- Beanbag chairs and other comfortable seating options
- Fidget tools, plush toys, and other focus aids
- Weighted items and other deep touch pressure inputs

One specific type of calming sensory room is called a Snoezelen® Multisensory Environment. Designed for use in hospitals and other clinical settings as an alternative to restraint and seclusion, Snoezelen rooms are starting to become more common as a calming solution in schools as well (Snoezelen.info, 2025).

Custom designed to meet each school's needs and preferences, Snoezelen® rooms are relaxing environments that help reduce anxiety while also engaging and stimulating users. Usually featuring gentle lighting, soothing sounds, and relaxing smells and textures, these rooms are purposefully furnished to promote calming and self-regulation, the very needs that seclusion is supposed to address (but often does not).

Some of the elements commonly found in these spaces include:

- Lighting effects that promote relaxation and therapy
- Bubble tubes that both calm and stimulate students
- Fiber optic products that transmit visually stimulating light signals
- Weighted blankets and other items that help students who need more sensory input
- Interactive panels that offer tactile, cause-and-effect stimulation, as well as visual, auditory, and/or aromatic experiences

One of the key characteristics of a Snoezelen® room is the use of sensory inputs designed to promote choice and independence by giving children a sense of control. For instance, giant wall pads called "Bumpas" not only act as padding to keep students safe; they also provide rich sensory feedback and stimulation by turning the wall into a rainbow-colored xylophone that students can "play" by touching each pad. Elements like these help students feel in control of their environment, which promotes self-regulation skills (Snoezelen.info, 2025).

Research supports the effectiveness of Snoezelen rooms as an alternative to seclusion or restraints in other settings, such as psychiatric facilities and even prisons. In one study of the use of Snoezelen rooms in a psychiatric setting (Teitelbaum et al., 2007), the researchers concluded that this type of environment "calms and relaxes agitative patients, giving them a feeling of dignity, initiative, and freedom of choice." Use **Tool 7.2: Planning Worksheet for Creating Spaces** to begin your brainstorming about the specialty spaces you may want to include in your school.

Figure 7.13

A Snoezelen® Multi-Sensory Environment Room is a Tool a School Can Provide for Students to Self-Regulate. This Computer Rendering Shows One Example of This Type of Room

Credit: School Specialty

Tool 7.2

PLANNING WORKSHEET FOR CREATING SPACES

Define the objective, instructional vision, and purpose for this space.	Objective: Instructional Vision: Purpose:
Identify core features that must be in this space.	
How will you address inclusivity in this space?	
Culture How will you make your media center an open and inviting space that students and teachers will want to use? How will you attract people to the space?	
Tools and furnishings What technology tools will be used in your media center? How will you support these tools with sufficient power and other infrastructure needs?	
Seating What types of seating do you envision for your media center?	
Community use Will your space be open to the community for use after school hours? How might spaces for large group instruction double as gathering places for staff, parents, or community members?	

••• REFLECTION QUESTIONS

1. How can the design of specialized learning environments like CTE classrooms, media centers, and sensory rooms enhance student engagement and learning outcomes?
2. In what ways can schools integrate flexible and adaptable furniture into media centers and CTE classrooms to accommodate evolving learning needs?
3. How do sensory spaces, including Snoezelen rooms, contribute to student well-being, and what elements are essential for creating an effective sensory environment? ●

Takeaways

1. **Specialized learning spaces must be purposefully designed** to support the unique needs of students, whether they are engaging in career and technical education, collaborative media projects, or self-regulation in sensory rooms.
2. **Flexibility is key in modern learning spaces**, with adaptable furniture, mobile storage, and multipurpose zones playing a crucial role in accommodating diverse learning activities.
3. **Sensory environments support student mental health and engagement**, providing necessary spaces for emotional regulation and focus, which ultimately contribute to a more inclusive and effective learning environment.

CHAPTER

8

SUPPORTING A CULTURE OF CONTINUOUS LEARNING AND SUCCESS

In this chapter, I will explore how school planners, designers, and administrators can take the concepts discussed previously and apply them to noninstructional spaces to extend learning and promote socialization and student wellness throughout the building.

Wouldn't it be amazing if students continued to discuss the topic they just learned once they left the classroom? Or if they were so engaged by that period's lesson that they kept working on their own or in groups with their friends, well after the bell rang?

It is what every teacher hopes for when they draw up a lesson plan. And while the quality of the instruction and the interest level of the learning materials play a key role in whether or not this happens, the physical environment also matters, as these continuous learning opportunities are much more likely to occur if your school building is designed to support them effectively.

If you limit your concept of a learning space only to classrooms, you are missing out on the chance to extend learning throughout the building—and the school day.

If you limit your concept of a learning space only to classrooms, you are missing out on the chance to extend learning throughout the building—and the school day. With the right design elements, *any* school space can support and even encourage rich student inquiry, reflection, communication, and collaboration.

If your building is designed to support and encourage learning beyond the classroom, then students might benefit from additional conversations and reflection about what they just learned in class. If not, then they are likely to pass on this opportunity and move on to thinking about something else.

Noninstructional spaces such as cafeterias, common areas, and outdoor spaces can serve as extensions of the learning that occurs in classrooms, thereby supporting a culture of continuous learning and reflection. However, this is more likely to happen if these spaces are equipped with comfortable, versatile furniture and tools that support continuous learning.

LEARNING BEYOND THE CLASSROOM

Integrating the School Specialty Six Essential Design Elements® I mentioned in Chapter 6 can help turn noninstructional spaces into places where learning continues beyond the classroom. Here is how.

Comfort: For students to continue the learning that just occurred in class, they need attractive and easily accessible places to sit down and talk, read, study, or look up information. These spaces, which can be hallways, large common areas, or even outdoor spaces, should be furnished with comfortable, appealing seating that draws students into the space and encourages them to stay and talk or do work between classes or after school.

Choice: Ideally, students will have different types of seating to choose from in hallways, common areas, and outdoor spaces, so they can "find their place" where they are most comfortable. Students are more likely to continue academic conversations or reflect on what they have learned if they have a comfortable place to stop, sit, and relax after class, complete with choices that allow them to feel like the space is their own. Do not discount outdoor spaces as alternative learning spaces (see Figures 8.1-8.3).

Connection: Learning is largely a social activity, and K–12 leaders should create opportunities for students to gather in small groups, hang out, and engage in informal learning in small groups when they are not in the classroom. Using soft lounge seating or café-style tables and chairs can make these areas communal gathering spaces where students enjoy spending time and making connections with each other (see Figure 8.4).

Figure 8.1

Outdoor Collaborative Learning

Credit: iStock.com/aldomurillo

Figure 8.2

Reading Outside

Credit: iStock.com/Mongkolchon Akesin

Figure 8.3

Outdoor Instruction Time

Credit: iStock.com/stevecoleimages

Figure 8.4

An Extended Learning Space Designed for Individuals and Small Groups

Credit: MooreCo Inc.

Flexibility: Informal learning spaces should be multipurpose spaces that can support different kinds of activities and interactions. Some students may prefer to sit and read by themselves, for instance, while others may choose to talk or work together in pairs or small groups. Equipping these spaces with a variety of furniture types—or with agile, modular furniture that can be configured in multiple ways—allows for many uses.

> **"Classroom furniture that serves different functions allows schools to invest in furniture and classroom design knowing it's not going to become obsolete in a few years."**
>
> (Ballegeer, 2024)

Stimulation: Students are most likely to use non-instructional spaces as extensions of the classroom if they feel inspired to continue their learning. While much of that depends on the quality of instruction they receive in class, schools can help foster a continuous learning culture by making informal learning spaces intellectually engaging and stimulating. For example, use furnishings, decorations, and age-appropriate tools or manipulatives that inspire curiosity in hallways and other common areas. Objects such as globes, maps, artwork, inventions, shelves of books, posters, inspiring quotes, dioramas, and displays of student work can encourage students to continually think, reflect, and explore.

Technology: For learning to happen anytime, anywhere, students need tools and materials to support their learning. These might be high-tech tools such as laptops, tablets, and interactive displays—or low-tech tools such as whiteboards or writable surfaces for students to jot down their ideas. While digital devices bring an entire world of information to students' fingertips, allowing students to learn from wherever they are, a dead battery renders this advantage useless. If you want noninstructional spaces to support continuous learning effectively, consider how these spaces will meet students' power needs with strategically placed electrical outlets—such as outlets embedded within tables, chairs, and other furniture.

SUPPORTING CONTINUOUS LEARNING IN SCHOOL COMMON AREAS

School hallways, foyers, and other common areas are often underutilized spaces that hold great potential for extending student learning. If you have room, add in hangout spots for students to congregate between classes or before and after school. If equipped with the right furniture and tools, these spaces can serve a wide variety of educational purposes.

For instance, students and teachers can use them as breakout spaces or extensions of the classroom, where groups of students might retreat to work on projects during class time. Students could also use these spaces for studying, tutoring, socializing, or independent reading—the possibilities are nearly endless.

Because these are often highly trafficked areas, choose durable furniture with easily washable fabrics when furnishing them. To maximize the utility of these spaces, make sure you provide a variety of seating styles—or use modular furniture that students can pull apart to sit by themselves or move together to work in pairs or small groups.

DESIGNING CAFETERIAS TO SUPPORT INFORMAL LEARNING

School and district leaders often take the design of their school cafeterias for granted. As a result, these spaces tend to feel very institutional and uninspiring.

But that is a big mistake. School cafeterias are places where everyone comes together during the school day. They represent a key opportunity to inspire school pride and a sense of community among students—and the design of the space can help foster this spirit.

School cafeterias can also become more functional by supporting learning activities when they are not being used for food service, such as after-school clubs or tutoring. Here is some advice for creating school cafeterias that are places students

Figure 8.5

Enjoyable School Cafeterias as Alternative Learning Areas

Credit: iStock.com/SDI Productions

want to spend time in, leading to a stronger sense of community and more opportunities for learning.

Get Rid of the Institutional Look and Feel

Students are subconsciously comparing your cafeteria to their favorite retail food chains when they are dining, and too often, the cafeteria comes up short. Consider replacing traditional picnic-style seating with seating you might see in a restaurant or café—booths, high-top tables, and comfortable café-style seating—to make the space more inviting and functional for both dining and collaboration.

I worked with one principal who recognized this challenge and transformed her school's cafeteria into a vibrant, student-friendly space. They partnered with a furniture dealer that offered a three-year phased-in plan. They also secured a grant focused on improving student wellness, which covered ergonomic seating designed to foster social interaction.

Similarly, another principal leveraged a combination of PTA fundraising and community partnerships to revamp the school's dining area. They launched a 'sponsor a seat' campaign, in which local businesses contributed to new café-style tables in exchange for small recognition plaques. This approach made the project affordable while building community engagement.

By exploring creative funding solutions—such as grants, local partnerships, and phased implementation—schools can reimagine their cafeterias as dynamic spaces that encourage both social connection and academic collaboration.

Think Creatively

When designing your cafeteria, take inspiration from restaurants, cafes, and other food-service venues. How can you increase food-service revenue while making your cafeteria an attractive place to be at? Could you create a food court or use self-service kiosks to lend a more modern feel to your dining programs, while also increasing the options available for students? How about a cafe-style section with coffee and pastries for older students? Giving students a variety of seating styles to choose from, including restaurant-style booths and smaller, cafe-style tables, helps students find spaces where they can be comfortable in the cafeteria (see Figure 8.6).

Power the Space for Learning

To make the space functional for learning or studying, consider how you can make electrical outlets readily available for students to plug in their digital devices. For instance, you could

Figure 8.6

A Design for a Welcoming Cafeteria

Credit: School Specialty

embed outlets in the floor or choose tables and bench seating with outlets built into the furniture.

Explore Ways to Reduce Noise

When you reduce the amount of noise in the space, it is easier for students to read, study, or even have meaningful conversations with each other. Fix the space, not the student interaction. Students need to be social during this time because they need that downtime to interact with other students. Baffles in the ceiling and acoustic tiles on the walls can help reduce noise levels in these spaces.

Look for Ways to Promote Connection

Create connections between students by using furniture that makes natural connections, such as round tables, tall seating options, soft setting areas, or booths. Add something special such as storage that can hold art materials or games, so students can enjoy this type of activity with friends. This is not just an activity for elementary students, but a way for middle and high school students to connect with one another as well (see Figure 8.7).

Figure 8.7

Cafeterias Designed for Student Connection

Credit: School Specialty

EXTENDING LEARNING OUTDOORS

Outdoor spaces offer many opportunities to extend student learning, and research suggests there are both educational and health-related benefits to learning outdoors.

Breathing fresh air can clear students' minds and help them think by increasing the amount of oxygen their brains receive. Being outside can also reduce stress and improve students' emotional well-being. In addition, exposure to natural sunlight helps prevent vitamin D deficiency—making students less vulnerable to bone problems, cardiovascular disease, diabetes, and other health issues. Additionally, research has shown that children with ADHD respond positively to spending time in natural settings (Taylor & Kuo, 2004). Taking students outdoors to participate in lessons is a no cost solution to begin your outdoor learning. Figure 8.8 is a computer rendering showing weather-resistant soft seating, tables, and chairs that can transform an outdoor courtyard or patio into a learning space.

Figure 8.8

Outdoor Spaces Designed for Learning and Connection

Credit: School Specialty

One study from the University of Illinois at Urbana-Champaign found that students paid more attention in class after an outdoor lesson (Browning & Penner, 2018). Other studies have linked outdoor learning to reduced stress, more enjoyment of school, and longer retention of information.

Educators can take advantage of outdoor settings to teach students about subjects like science or conservation in a hands-on manner. Nature walks, collection or measurement stations, working gardens, and greenhouses are all scenarios in which students can engage in applied learning, observing the effects of nature first-hand. One successful example of a school garden is Maytree Nursery School and Children's Centre in Lambeth, which transformed a small garden around the Children's Centre into an engaging and creative school growing space. The aim was to create a learning environment where children and families could grow plants together, encouraging skills such as planning and nurturing, as well as collaboration (Greater London Authority, 2016). See examples of outdoor learning in Figures 8.9 and 8.10.

Alternatively, outdoor spaces can simply be places where students have a chance to sit outside and learn, socialize, eat, relax, or work collaboratively. Outdoor classrooms can be a fun change of pace for students and a great way for teachers to bring a twist to their lessons. This might happen within an outdoor patio, courtyard, pavilion, or other space.

Figure 8.9

Elementary Science

Credit: iStock.com/orafotograf

Figure 8.10

Elementary School Engineering

Credit: iStock.com/fstop123

When furnishing outdoor learning spaces, use furniture that is weather-resistant and designed for outdoor use. Fabrics can retain moisture and are most effective if the space is sheltered from rain. Also, be sure to add shade structures to protect students from the sun and other elements.

To support effective outdoor learning, you will need external spaces that are intentionally designed for success. Here are some questions to consider.

- ***Users***: What grade levels will be using outdoor learning spaces, and what age-appropriate furnishings and equipment are required?
- ***Purposes***: Will these spaces be used for instruction, recreation or both? What do you hope to accomplish with these spaces?
- ***Learning goals***: What classes and subject areas will use outdoor learning spaces for instruction? What types of learning activities will take place there, and what furniture, equipment and materials will this require?

Figure 8.11 is a computer rendering showing an example of comfortable and attractive places to sit and gather outdoors before and after school or during lunch breaks.

Figure 8.11

Outdoor Seating

Credit: School Specialty

MAKING EVERY SPACE COUNT

Funding can be tricky, but there are many creative solutions beyond a bond or referendum. Districts and schools can look to the community for additional support, businesses can support new programs and spending general fund in small ways. You do not have to have millions of dollars to start the redesign of your learning environments. Begin by adding one or two alternative pieces of seating in a classroom, move your current furniture around, or even have teachers trade furniture. You can also start by trying some new instructional methods that encourage students to move around their current furniture.

To sum up, do not overlook the value of hallways, common areas, cafeterias, outdoor spaces, and other noninstructional spaces when designing and outfitting school buildings. With the right equipment, furniture, and a little creativity, every single square foot of a school can support student learning. Spaces outside the regular classroom can make an impact on students such as The Cherish Center wellness room. This sensory room at the United Independent School District in Texas has helped students, particularly those with special needs, by reducing anxiety, improving behavior, and preparing them for learning. (School Specialty, 2025a) Another success story is Stroudsburg High School. Key areas of focus were creating dynamic, student-centered spaces, such as a modernized library for collaboration and a vibrant cafeteria. The project successfully enhanced both technical and academic spaces, with feedback from the community highlighting its positive impact. (School Specialty, n.d.)

> **Cabrillo High School, in Lompoc, California, had a vision in the late 1980s to create and build an aquatics program. It all began a club, not a full aquarium. This program began with donations from the community of used fishtanks, fish, and supplies. Students raised money through fundraising. The program began in an unused classroom with folding tables as stands.**
>
> **Over the years, they have written numerous grants, applied for contests, applied for grant money through federal programs, and continued to raise money in creative ways. Today, they have a standalone aquarium building and have made it into a beautiful place for the public and other students to tour. This was not a short journey with all funds raised all in one year, but over many years**
>
> (Cabrillo High School Aquarium, 2022).

Reflect on the use of noninstructional spaces in your school by responding to the prompts in **Tool 8: Brainstorming Prompts for Noninstructional Spaces**.

Tool 8

BRAINSTORMING PROMPTS FOR NONINSTRUCTIONAL SPACES

Outdoor spaces

Cafeteria

Common spaces

Hallways

Others

Define the objective and purpose for this space. How will the space be used before, during, and after school?	
Identify core features that must be in this space.	
How will you address inclusivity in this space?	
How will you address acoustics in this space or weather if it is outside?	
What is the budget for this space?	
Who will be using this space and when?	
Visualize your space: • Sketch your ideal design for the space, labeling key areas and features. • Create an instructional vision board with images, materials, and ideas. • Use sticky notes or a digital brainstorming tool to organize ideas by priority.	

••• REFLECTION QUESTIONS

1. How can the design of noninstructional spaces in your school be improved to better support student learning, socialization, and well-being?
2. In what ways do the six essential design elements—comfort, choice, connection, flexibility, stimulation, and technology—enhance continuous learning beyond the classroom?
3. How could your school's cafeteria, hallways, or outdoor spaces be transformed to encourage student collaboration and engagement outside of traditional class time? ●

Key Takeaways

1. Noninstructional spaces, such as cafeterias, hallways, and outdoor areas, can serve as extensions of the classroom by fostering continued learning, reflection, and social interaction.
2. Integrating elements like comfortable seating, technology access, and flexible design encourages students to engage in academic conversations and collaborative work beyond structured class time.
3. Outdoor learning environments provide numerous cognitive and health benefits, enhancing student focus, reducing stress, and supporting hands-on learning experiences in subjects like science and environmental studies.

CHAPTER 9

MAKING A PLAN TO TRANSFORM YOUR SCHOOL ENVIRONMENT

Whether you are a teacher, building administrator, district administrator, or a purchasing agent, using the tools in this book will help you to design your roadmap for success. Begin at Chapter 1 with the readiness rubric to make sure you determine if you are ready for change. From there, use the tools in each chapter to help you plan and prepare your new environments. This chapter is designed to help you create the final step, the implementation plan for your new learning environments.

If there is a message I would like to leave readers with, it is that learning environments are critical elements in supporting both high-quality instruction *and* student and staff wellness. By integrating elements such as choice, comfort, and flexibility into learning environments, we can meet students where they are more effectively. The bottom line is, there is no "one-size-fits-all" approach in education—and this applies to students, to instruction, and to the learning environments that support these.

Designing modern learning environments that support active and collaborative learning as well as social-emotional needs such as inclusion and connectedness can happen at any stage. It can be part of the planning process for a new building or renovation project, or it can be undertaken on a piecemeal basis. It does not have to be a costly undertaking, either: Even small changes made by principals or individual teachers to their learning spaces can have a big impact.

Transforming learning environments can be achieved successfully if planned with a clear vision and strategies across a school or district (see Figure 9.1). Implementing new environments is not easy, but it can be done effectively if you follow a few proven processes. Whether you are a teacher trying to implement a new classroom environment or a district implementing a refresh program, here are some suggestions to guide you. Whether you ae a teacher, building administrator, district administrator, or a purchasing agent, using the tools in this book will help you to design your roadmap for success. Begin at Chapter 1 with the readiness rubric to make sure you determine if you are ready for change. From there, use the tools in each chapter to help you plan and prepare your new environments. This chapter is designed to help you create the final step, the implementation plan for your new learning environments.

TEACHER IMPLEMENTATION

First, congratulations on wanting to try something new and different! This means you want to improve your instruction and take it to the next level.

If you are a teacher looking to make changes in your own classroom, I would recommend that you start small and build from there. For instance, think about giving students choices in where they sit during instruction or in how they create groups for small group work. You might also consider adding in some alternative seating in your classroom. This could include floor cushions, bean bag chairs, or wobble stools. Wobble stools and other seats that allow for student movement without disrupting instruction are powerful tools for students who have attention challenges. This movement actually helps them to pay attention or concentrate on a task.

Other small steps you can take include arranging seating to encourage collaboration whenever it makes sense in the learning process, allowing for movement during class, and adding design elements that stimulate thought and discussion. If you do not have a budget from your school or district to make these types of changes, look for alternative seating options at discount furniture stores or seek donations from families.

Figure 9.1

Examples of Clear Visions From K–12 Districts

Galt Joint Union Elementary School District (California)

Vision Statement:

"Our schools create safe learning environments that provide equitable access to engaging opportunities for all children. We foster learning environments for collaboration, creativity, and critical thinking to ensure children are successful in school and in their future." (Galt Joint Union Elementary School District, 2025)

Weston Public Schools (Massachusetts)

Vision Statement:

"Students will imagine, reflect, and innovate within a safe, equitable, and responsive learning environment that develops their academic, social, and emotional growth and holistic well-being." (Weston Public Schools, 2025)

Implementation Ideas for Teachers

- **Offer seating choices**: Allow students to choose where they sit during instruction to give them more autonomy over their learning environment.
- **Create flexible grouping**: Let students decide how they want to form groups for small group work, fostering collaboration and a sense of ownership in their learning.
- **Introduce alternative seating**: Add seating options like floor cushions, bean bag chairs, or wobble stools to support diverse learning styles and promote comfort.
- **Arrange seating for collaboration**: Reorganize desks or tables to encourage group work and collaboration, especially when group activities align with the lesson plan.
- **Encourage movement**: Provide opportunities for students to move around the classroom, whether through movement breaks or allowing them to stand or stretch during lessons.

(Continued)

(Continued)

- **Add stimulating design elements:** Incorporate décor, posters, or artwork that sparks thought and conversation, creating an inspiring and engaging atmosphere.
- **Seek affordable seating options:** If budget is a concern, explore affordable alternative seating from discount furniture stores or ask families for donations to improve the classroom environment.

SCHOOL IMPLEMENTATION

If you are a school administrator who wants to make some changes in your building, I would also recommend starting small. First, examine the instructional materials you use, the pedagogy you have implemented (or want to implement), and the readiness of your staff. Once you have gathered all of this information, try creating a small pilot group who would be willing to help plan, try out the changes, and give feedback on what is working well and what is not. These should be early adopters who are willing to step out of their comfort zones and try something new. You might also look to transform common areas and outdoor spaces into places that encourage more connection and continuous learning.

Change is difficult. When we ask our teachers to do something new, we need to be sure we are not saying that what they are doing now is terrible. Supporting teachers with ample professional development is also absolutely critical to the success of environment changes, just as it is in the implementation of a new curriculum. With a structured plan, you can make impactful and sustainable improvements that positively influence both teaching and learning. Begin by carefully evaluating the instructional materials currently in use, the pedagogical approaches being implemented (or those you wish to implement), and the readiness of your staff. Are they familiar with current practices? Are they open to new methodologies?

Despite common wisdom, I have found that starting with the "why" behind the changes is not always the most effective way to make change. I believe that starting with procedural changes helps with implementation because it is not personal, it is a process. When asking teachers to try something new, it is essential not to imply that what they are currently doing is inadequate or "wrong." Instead, emphasize that these changes are opportunities to enhance and support their existing practices. Teachers are incredibly dedicated, and it is important to support them with ample professional development to ensure the success of any new initiatives, just as you would for a new curriculum implementation.

> **"Over 80% [of students] reported high increase in creativity, motivation, ability to get higher grades and engagement in class while studying in the new learning environment."**
> (Scott-Webber et al., 2016)

Once people see how these changes connect with the instructional practices, then you can return to the "why." I have seen this happen time and time again with environment implementation, because it is not a set of curriculum materials that has a clear plan or map connected. An environment change is more nebulous and can involve strong emotions. There is no corresponding map to show you how to use it, which is why professional learning is even more critical.

If a school or district is changing their learning environments in a significant way, professional learning is critical. It may seem silly to think leaders need to teach the "how to" for a piece of furniture, but it is not. Teachers need to understand the "why" behind the furniture choices, the connection to instruction, and how to change the environment to meet the needs of their students. A structured professional learning plan for environment changes might look something like this:

- **Understanding the Instructional Vision for Our District:** Help staff understand the overall vision for learning in your district and how the physical environment plays a crucial role in supporting this vision.
- **Our School/District Vision for Learning Environments:** Explain how this connects directly to your instructional vision and why these changes are necessary for student success.
- **Rationale for Furniture Choices:** Share the process behind selecting new classroom furniture, explaining how the design fosters flexible learning environments that support different teaching styles.
- **Connecting Furniture to Instructional Strategies:** Demonstrate how teachers can use new furniture arrangements to support various instructional strategies, such as project-based learning, student collaboration, or differentiated instruction.
- **Sample Room Layouts:** Provide examples of different classroom layouts that use the new furniture and how these configurations can enhance learning activities.

Implementation Steps for School Administrators

- **Start small**: Begin by evaluating instructional materials, pedagogy, and staff readiness. Identify areas for improvement.
- **Create a pilot group**: Establish a small group of early adopters who are open to trying new approaches, providing feedback on what works and what needs adjustment.
- **Transform common areas and outdoor spaces**: Redesign shared spaces like hallways, cafeterias, and outdoor areas first to impact the largest number of students.
- **Evaluate the "how" before the "why"**: When introducing changes, start with practical, procedural adjustments rather than focusing initially on the underlying philosophy. This allows teachers to ease into changes without feeling their current practices are being undermined.
- **Communicate the connection between environment changes and instructional practices**: Once teachers are familiar with the practical aspects of the changes, explain the rationale behind them, linking the changes to the broader instructional goals.
- **Provide ongoing professional learning**: Develop a structured plan for professional development that includes:
  - Understanding the district's instructional vision and its connection to the learning environment.
  - Ensure staff understands how changes in the physical environment can foster better engagement, collaboration, and overall student learning, rather than merely focusing on aesthetics or novelty.
  - Demonstrating how new furniture arrangements support instructional strategies like project-based learning or collaboration.
  - Providing sample classroom layouts to show how furniture can enhance various learning activities.
- **Create feedback loops**: Regularly collect feedback from teachers and students about the changes and use this information to make necessary adjustments, ensuring the environment evolves to meet the needs of all learners.

By focusing on these actionable steps and addressing teachers' needs through structured support and professional learning, administrators can ensure that changes to the learning environment are implemented successfully and have a lasting positive impact on both students and staff. You will find a useful tool at the end of this chapter that can be modified for a school level change.

DISTRICT IMPLEMENTATION

If you are a district administrator looking to refresh your learning environments or implement all-new environments, then the process takes a bit longer. I have included a planning tool at the end of this chapter to help you plan for full-scale implementation. Again, begin with a small planning group who can help provide input throughout the planning process.

Once you have used the tools in this book to evaluate readiness (Tools 1, 3, and 5), brainstorm goals and your instructional vision (Tools 2.1 and 2.2), decide on the scope of your project (Tool 4), evaluate your current environment (Tool 6), and plan your new spaces (Tools 7.1, 7.2, and 8), you can use the following process (Tool 9) to help evaluate and implement your new learning environments. Pilot programs are not essential, but districts often implement them to test new learning spaces. These pilot programs might involve a couple of individual classrooms, or they might include a training room or two where teachers will learn about the new environments and do professional development in those spaces to learn how to use these new tools in their instruction. One note of caution about having just one or two teachers evaluate and pilot a new classroom environment: This does not give the larger teacher and administrative pool an opportunity to see, touch, and try out the new spaces as easily as if it were in a shared space.

TOOLKITS FOR THE CLASSROOM

I like to think of an educator's metaphorical toolkit as the sum of all resources that a teacher brings to his or her interactions with students. This toolkit is unique to every district, school, and teacher. It consists of the personal knowledge, experience, interests, and strategies that educators possess, as well as the design of the learning environment and the curriculum, supplies, infrastructure, and supports that teachers have access to.

Everyone's toolkit will look different, and that is OK. The toolkit of a 20-year veteran teacher is very different from that of a teacher in her second year. But as we continue to recover from the trauma of the pandemic and look ahead to the future, it is important for teachers and administrators to reassess their toolkits and think about what elements they might want to add or change. Consider using the learning environment as an additional tool for your toolkit.

What has worked well for you in the past? What did not work so well—and what can you learn from this experience? Are there any supplies, technologies, furnishings, or materials you wish you had that might have made instruction easier? What will you need to meet students' academic and social-emotional needs more effectively moving forward?

Each teacher's "toolkit" should take into account many factors, including students' grade levels, strengths, needs, interests, demographics, curricular focus, and school or district focus. The learning environment can provide that equity and access, for every teacher and student, to a set of tools that will provide a future-ready space for students to be successful and healthy.

In **Tool 9: Steps for a Learning Environment Pilot**, you will find steps for planning, piloting (trying out), and implementing new learning environments. These steps list several activities that should be considered throughout the process of implementation. Before you begin a large overhaul of your environments or a small refresh, you will want to have a plan in place to ensure all stakeholders have a voice in the process.

FINAL THOUGHTS ON IMPLEMENTATION

Ultimately, the transformation of learning environments is a journey, not a destination. Whether implementing small changes in an individual classroom or undertaking a large-scale district-wide initiative, the key to success lies in thoughtful planning, ongoing collaboration, and a commitment to continuous improvement. By fostering a culture of innovation and adaptability, schools can create environments that truly support students' learning, engagement, and well-being. As you move forward, remember that every step—no matter how small—is a step toward a more effective and inclusive learning space for all.

Tool 9

STEPS TO PROGRESS FROM LEARNING ENVIRONMENT PILOT TO FULL IMPLEMENTATION

Goals:

- Evaluate different elements within the learning environment and gain insights
- Enhance teacher satisfaction in classroom form and function
- Allow all stakeholders the opportunity to contribute to learning environment design
- Collect data to inform implementation decisions

STEPS		DATES (IF APPLICABLE)
1.Planning & research (To be completed before kickoff meeting)	• **Establish Project Team**: Include school leadership, teachers, IT staff, facilities management, and student representatives. • **Research Best Practices**: Examine case studies of innovative learning environments and align with emerging trends (e.g., flexible seating, collaborative spaces, technology integration, and sensory-friendly zones). • **Define Success Criteria**: Set clear metrics for evaluating the pilot (e.g., student engagement, teacher satisfaction, tech utilization, and impact on learning). • **Budget**: determine budget for the project	
2. Kickoff meeting	• **Assess Needs**: Conduct surveys, focus groups, and walkthroughs to identify current gaps and aspirations. • **Share**: research about learning space best practices • **Define**: success metrics as a group	Date for kickoff meeting:
3. Decide if you will use a pilot classroom(s) for testing.	• **Select** pilot classroom(s)/ area(s) • **Inform** teachers/ administration	Date for pilot classroom decision:

(Continued)

(Continued)

4. Walk through current learning environments	Visit current classrooms with the project team to identify the following about the environments: • Important: List essential furniture • Occasional Use: Identify pieces of occasional utility • Not Needed: Assess pieces that do not meet needs • Wish List: Create a wish list of items you would really like to have.	Date of walkthrough:
5. Initial design meeting	Create the classroom design and gather input from stakeholder team: • Conduct an initial design meeting with the furniture vendor to review instructional vision, project design concepts, color palettes, and product options.	Date of design meeting:
6. Pilot dates - optional: (Suggested time: minimum of one semester)	Determine when you want to conduct a pilot classroom program. This is where a few teachers (1 to 5) will try out your initial room design using the furniture in their classrooms for a semester. (Note: This step can be skipped. It is not always required.)	Dates of your pilot program:
7. Check in: Have a mid-semester and end of semester design meeting to gather feedback	Mid-pilot: gather feedback, what is working and what is not working	Date of design usage meeting (mid-semester):
	End of pilot: gather feedback, what worked, what did not work, what pieces would you change • Analyze feedback/data from pilot • Adjust design and implementation plan • Present findings to stakeholders	Date of design usage meeting (end-of-semester):

8. Final design meeting	Conduct a final design meeting to make any final changes to the learning environment.	Date of design meeting:
9. Finalize installation and implementation plans for the project.	Complete . . . • Installation plans with furniture company • Final punch list walkthrough • Roll out refreshed environments in phases	Date when final installation and implementation will be completed:
9. Install and implement your new environments.	• Provide ongoing training and coaching on the care and use of their new learning environments. • Track long-term results	Dates for training days: Dates for periodically assessing results:

CATEGORY	DETAILS / TO BE COMPLETED BY
Budget Estimates	• COO, Superintendent, and Bond committee
Pilot Evaluation Criteria	• Stakeholder team, Curriculum Department, and Superintendent
Stakeholder Engagement Plan	• Planning team and Superintendent
Professional Development Needs	• During planning • After installation • Ongoing support
Communications Plan	• Internal Updates: Staff, stakeholder team • Parent & Community Engagement: Host open houses and publish newsletters. • Student Involvement: Share progress via student-led tours or school media.

CONCLUDING THOUGHTS AND FINAL TAKEAWAYS

Transforming your school's learning environment is an exciting and essential journey for improving teaching and learning, along with increasing retention of good teachers. The heart of this transformation lies in understanding the deep impact that well-designed spaces can have on student engagement, academic achievement, and overall well-being. As we have explored in this book, whether you are making small enhancements in a single classroom, changing a cafeteria to provide exciting gathering space, or leading a district-wide initiative, a thoughtful and systematic approach will help to ensure long-term success for all. Remember, this is not a quick fix or magic bullet, but one that can have sustained impact for students and teachers.

Today's students are growing up in a world that demands more support, more flexibility, and more intentional approaches to teaching and learning than ever before—and our learning environments must evolve to meet those needs. I am calling on school leaders, educators, communities, and policymakers to work together in transforming schools into spaces that nurture the whole child—not just academically, but socially, emotionally, and physically.

Key Takeaways

1. **Start Small, Think Big:** You do not need a complete overhaul to make a meaningful impact. Begin with small changes—like providing flexible seating options or rearranging classroom layouts—to create a more dynamic, collaborative, and engaging learning environment. These small shifts can lead to big results in terms of student engagement and academic success and help build support for future initiatives.
2. **Plan, Pilot, and Evaluate:** Whether you are a teacher, school leader, or district administrator, developing a clear and achievable plan is essential for success. Start with a small group, gather feedback, and refine your approach based on what works and what does not. Consider implementing a pilot plan for more substantive feedback. This iterative process helps to minimize risks while ensuring that your changes meet the needs of both students and teachers.
3. **Support Teachers Through Professional Learning:** Any change in the learning environment must be accompanied by well-planned professional development. Teachers need to understand not just how to use new furniture or classroom layouts, but also the deeper "why" behind these changes. This understanding is essential for making the most out of the new environments and enriching instructional practices.
4. **Involve Stakeholders:** Transformation is most successful when it is inclusive of different voices. Engage teachers, students, parents, and other stakeholders in the planning process. Their input is invaluable for creating spaces that are not only functional but also supportive of diverse learning needs.
5. **Address the Social-Emotional Needs of Students:** Modern learning environments must support not only academic growth but also social-emotional well-being. Consider how your changes can foster inclusion, equity, and connection, ensuring that all students feel safe, valued, and capable of thriving.
6. **Commit to Continuous Improvement:** The journey to transform learning environments is ongoing. As needs evolve and new insights emerge, it is important to revisit your plans and refine them. By committing to continuous improvement, schools can stay responsive to the changing needs of students, educators, and the broader community. Be sure to include ongoing coaching and support for new teachers as they enter into these new environments.

Ultimately, the transformation of your school's learning environment is an opportunity to reimagine what education and education spaces can look like, sound like, and feel like. By taking a thoughtful, collaborative approach, you can create spaces that are not only conducive to learning but also foster creativity, connection, and the holistic development of every student. This process, though challenging at times, pays off in the long run—empowering both students and educators to thrive in dynamic, engaging, and supportive environments.

As we have explored throughout *Reimagining Learning Spaces: Designing Educational Environments for a New Generation*, meaningful change happens when we intentionally move past traditional boundaries and embrace a broader vision of what schools can be. School leaders lead innovation and redesign implementation by creating a culture that asks how educational environments can better meet the needs of students and teachers. Educators who use these

(Continued)

(Continued)

spaces on a daily basis need to be encouraged to contribute their insights, expertise, and voice to designing and transforming these spaces to meet the ever-evolving needs of students. Encourage your community members and local businesses to contribute their resources and expertise into reimagining your learning environments. Share the needs of your students with community members, thereby inviting them to step up to support your efforts. Hold your policy makers accountable for aligning funding and legislation to support your professional development needs and the needs of your school and district. Success requires the collective efforts of all interested parties working together to create environments that lead to improved well-being and that foster creativity and deeper learning in students.

As you continue this journey, remember: every step forward—no matter how small—is a step towards reimagining a better future and toward unlocking the full potential of every learner. Together, we can create learning environments where teachers and students alike flourish, where education is reimagined, and where the future of learning is built with intention, compassion, and bold vision.

The time is now. Let us move forward—bravely and collaboratively—to create schools that do not just educate, but truly empower every learner, every educator, and every future.

REFERENCES

Advance CTE. (2023). *CTE in your state.* Retrieved from https://careertech.org/our-vision/cte-in-your-state/

Association of Supervision and Curriculum Development. (2007). *The learning compact redefined: A call to action.* http://ascd.org/learningcompact.

Ballegeer, B. (2024). The effects of furniture in today's classroom are far-ranging. *GBD Magazine.* https://gbdmagazine.com/classroom-furniture-effects/

Bandura, A. (1986). *Social foundations of thought and action: A social cognitive theory.* Prentice-Hall.

Bandura, A. (1977). Self-efficacy: toward a unifying theory of behavioral change. *Psychological Review, 84,* 19–1215.

Bandura, A. (1997). *Self-efficacy: The exercise of control.* W.H. Freeman.

Barnum, M. (2023, March 6). Teacher turnover hits new highs across the U.S. *Chalkbeat.* https://www.chalkbeat.org/2023/3/6/23624340/teacher-turnover-leaving-the-profession-quitting-higher-rate/

Barraza, L. (2021). Designing learning spaces that inspire: How classroom aesthetics impact student motivation. *Learning Environments Research, 24*(2), 245–258. https://doi.org/10.1007/s10984-021-09353-7

Barrett, P., Davies, F., Zhang, Y., & Barrett, L. (2015). *Clever classrooms: Summary report of the HEAD Project.* University of Salford.

Basdogan, M., & Morrone, A. S. (2021). Learning space matters: Student academic success in technology-enhanced active learning classrooms. *Journal of Learning Spaces, 10*(2), 1–12. https://libjournal.uncg.edu/jls/article/view/2233

Brodnitz, L. (2024, January 15). The most in-demand skills for 2024, according to LinkedIn data. *LinkedIn.* https://www.linkedin.com/pulse/most-demand-skills-2024-laurie-brodnitz

Brooks, D. C. (2012). Space and consequences: The impact of different formal learning spaces on instructor and student behavior. *Journal of Learning Spaces, 1*(2). https://libjournal.uncg.edu/jls/article/view/285

Browning, M., & Penner, M. (2018). School-based outdoor education and student attention: A systematic review of the literature. *Frontiers in Psychology, 8*, 2267. https://doi.org/10.3389/fpsyg.2017.02267

Cabrillo High School Aquarium. (2022). *About us.* Retrieved February 19, 2025, from https://www.cabrillohighschoolaquarium.org/about-us

Carver-Thomas, D., & Darling-Hammond, L. (2019). The trouble with teacher turnover: How teacher attrition affects students and schools. *Education Policy Analysis Archives, 27*(36).

CAST. (2018). *Universal design for learning guidelines version 2.2.* Retrieved from http://udlguidelines.cast.org

Centers for Disease Control and Prevention. (2024). *Peer connection and support.* U.S. Department of Health & Human Services. https://www.cdc.gov/classroom-management/approaches/peer-connection-support.html

Check & Connect. (2025). *Student Engagement Instrument (SEI).* University of Minnesota. Retrieved from https://checkandconnect.umn.edu/sei/default.html

Davis School District (2020, March 5). *Flexible seating supports learning first* [Video]. YouTube. https://youtu.be/VyiyKlD42-w.

Dewey, J. (1938). *Experience and education.* New York: Collier Books.

Edthena. (2023). The 4 things you should be looking for to measure student engagement. *Edthena.* Retrieved from https://www.edthena.com/4-ways-to-measure-student-engagement/

Fisher, D., & Frey, N. (2003). Writing instruction for struggling adolescent readers: A gradual release model. *Journal of Adolescent and Adult Literacy, 46*, 396–407.

Gallup. (2023). *Voices of Gen Z - Perspectives on U.S. education, well-being and the future.* Retrieved fromfile:///Users/highls66/Downloads/Gallup-Walton%20Family%20Foundation%20Voices%20of%20Gen%20Z%20Report%20(1).pdf.

Galt Joint Union Elementary School District. (2025). *Mission and vision statements.* Retrieved March 16, 2025, from https://www.galt.k12.ca.us/Our-District/Mission-and-Vision-Statements/index.html

Gao, N., Rahaman, M. S., Shao, W., Ji, K., & Salim, F. D. (2021). Individual and group-wise classroom seating experience: Effects on student engagement in different courses. *arXiv preprint arXiv:2112.12342.* https://doi.org/10.48550/arXiv.2112.12342

Greater London Authority. (2016). Maytree Nursery School and Children's Centre case study. Retrieved from https://www.london.gov.uk/sites/default/files/maytree_case_study.pdf

Guardino, C., & Fullerton, E. (2010). Changing behaviors by changing the classroom environment. *Teaching Exceptional Children, 42*(6), 8–13. https://doi.org/10.1177/004005991004200601

Hanover Research. (2021). *4 strategies to increase teacher retention.* Washington Association of School Administrators. Retrieved from https://wasa-oly.org/WASA/images/WASA/6.0%20Resources/Hanover/4%20STRATEGIES%20TO%20INCREASE%20TEACHER%20RETENTION.pdf

Harvey, B., & Kenyon, M. C. (2013). *Classroom design and student engagement.* University of Michigan Center for Research on Learning and Teaching. https://crlt.umich.edu/blog/classroom-design-and-student-engagement

Hattie, J. (2008). *Visible learning: A synthesis of over 800 meta-analyses relating to achievement.* Routledge.

Hattie, J., & Yates, G. C. R. (2014). *Visible learning and the science of how we learn.* Milton Park, Abingdon, Oxon; New York, Routledge.

Insight Education Group. (2020). *Teacher recruitment & retention playbook.* Effective Educator Development. Retrieved from https://eed.communities.ed.gov/sites/default/files/2024-07/Teacher%20Recruitment%20%26%20Retention.pdf

Institute for Local Government. (2014). *PBL essential elements checklist.* Retrieved from https://www.ca-ilg.org/sites/main/files/file-attachments/pbl_checklist.pdf

Kariippanon, K. E., Cliff, D. P., Lancaster, S. L., Okely, A. D., & Parrish, A. M. (2018). Perceived interplay between flexible learning spaces and teaching, learning and student wellbeing. *Learning Environments Research, 21*(3), 301–320.

Kepez, O., & Üst, S. (2024). Furniture configurations in an active learning classroom make further differences in student outcomes. *Archnet-IJAR, 18*(1), 121–141. https://doi.org/10.1108/arch-06-2022-0132

Killian, S. (2021, September 15). Top instructional strategies according to Hattie and Marzano. *McREL International.* https://www.mcrel.org/top-instructional-strategies-according-to-hattie-and-marzano/

Kuo, M., Browning, M. H., & Penner, M. L. (2018). Do lessons in nature boost subsequent classroom engagement? Refueling students in flight. *Frontiers in Psychology, 8*, 2253.

Lorsbach, A., & Jinks, J. (1999). Self-efficacy theory and learning environment research. *Learning Environments Research, 2*, 157–167.

Love, T., & Roy, K. (2022). *[Title of the report].* International Technology and Engineering Educators Association (ITEEA).

Makowski, M. (2017, August 18). GVSU study: activity-permissible classrooms lead to more student engagement. *GVNext.*

Marquez, J. (2019). The impact of classroom design on teachers and students. *Edutopia.* https://www.edutopia.org/article/impact-classroom-design-teachers-and-students

Maslow, A. H. (1943). A theory of human motivation. *Psychological Review, 50* (4), 370–396.

Maslow, A. H. (1972). *The farther reaches of human nature.* Viking Press.

Maslow, A. H. (1987). *Motivation and personality* (3rd ed.). Delhi, India: Pearson Education.

McMullen, M. (2022). Work-life balance is a myth: Three fundamental truths that will serve you better. *Forbes.* https://www.forbes.com/councils/forbesbusinesscouncil/2022/10/03/work-life-balance-is-a-myth-three-fundamental-truths-that-will-serve-you-better/

Merod, A. (2024, February 15). *The average school building is nearly a half-century old.* K–12 Dive. https://www.k12dive.com/news/public-school-infrastructure-age-nces/707580/

Mervosh, S., & Paris, F. (2024, February 27). *Chronic school absenteeism has 'exploded' since the pandemic.* The New York Times. https://www.nytimes.com/2024/02/27/us/school-absent-chronic-education.html

Miller, J. (2024). *Oregon student health survey highlights teen anxiety trends.* Oregon Department of Education.

Najarro, I. (2024, January 22). English learners now make up more than 10% of the nation's K-12 enrollment. *Education Week.* https://www.edweek.org/teaching-learning/english-learners-now-make-up-more-than-10-of-the-nations-k-12-enrollment/2024/01

OECD. (2018). *Results (Volume I). Teachers and school leaders as lifelong learners.* 2019. https://www.oecd.org/education/talis-2018-results

Pew Research Center. (2023, December 14). *Special education in the U.S. (2023).* Pew Research Center. https://www.pewresearch.org/short-reads/2023/12/14/special-education-in-the-us/

Phillips, D. C. (1995). The good, the bad, and the ugly: The many faces of constructivism. *Educational Researcher, 24* (7), 5–12.

Prochaska, J. O., & Velicer, W. F. (1997). The transtheoretical model of health behavior change. *American Journal of Health Promotion, 12*(1), 38–48.

Project Tomorrow. (2023). *Speak up research project for digital learning: 2023 findings.* Project Tomorrow. https://tomorrow.org/speakup/

Rands, M. L., & Gansemer-Topf, A. M. (2017). The room itself is active: How classroom design impacts student engagement. *Journal of Learning Spaces, 6*(1), 26–33.

Sadeghi, T., & Farahani, L. (2016). The impact of school furniture on fourth grade children's on-task and sitting behavior in the classroom: a pilot study. *Ergonomics, 59*(6), 800–808. https://doi.org/10.1080/00140139.2016.1188080

School Specialty. (n.d.). *Stroudsburg High School – Case study.* School Specialty. https://blog.schoolspecialty.com/stroudsburg-high-school-case-study/

School Specialty. (2025a). *Cherish Center case study.* School Specialty. Retrieved March 16, 2025, from https://blog.schoolspecialty.com/cherish-center-case-study/

School Specialty. (2025b). *When creating a vision for learning space design, here are six key factors to consider.* School Specialty. Retrieved February 1, 2025, from https://blog.schoolspecialty.com/when-creating-a-vision-for-learning-space-design-here-are-six-key-factors-to-consider/

School Specialty, LLC. (2025). *360 Philosophy.* www.schoolspecialty.com

Scott-Webber, L. (2014). *Rethinking spatial designs to support learning.* Academia.edu. https://www.academia.edu/39399528/Rethinking_Spatial_Designs_to_Support_Learning

Scott-Webber, L., Amar, S., Nissim, Y., & Weissblueth, E. (2016). The effect of a stimulating learning environment on pre-service teachers' motivation and 21st-century skills. *Journal of Education and Learning, 5*(3), 14–27.

Scott-Webber, L., Strickland, A., & Ringler, C. (2014). Built environments impact behaviors: Results of an active learning post-occupancy evaluation. *Planning for Higher Education, 42*(1), 41–57. ERIC. https://eric.ed.gov/?id=EJ1098636

Snoezelen.info. (2025). *Snoezelen multi-sensory environments.* Retrieved [date], from https://snoezelen.info/

Springtide Research Institute. (2024). *Thirteen: A first look at Gen Alpha.* Springtide Research Institute. https://springtideresearch.org/wp-content/uploads/2024/07/thirteen-a-first-look-at-gen-alpha-springtide-research-institute.pdf

Spyhalski, S. (2019). Sensory rooms helping students succeed in Muskegon County schools. *WGVU Public Media.* https://www.wgvunews.org/post/sensory-rooms-helping-students-succeed-muskegon-county-schools

Taylor, A. F., & Kuo, F. E. (2004). Children with attention deficits concentrate better after walk in the park. *American Journal of Public Health, 94*(9), 1580–1586. https://doi.org/10.2105/AJPH.94.9.1580

Teitelbaum, J., Voloshin, D., & Milgram, N. (2007). The use of Snoezelen in the management of aggression in psychiatric settings. *The International Journal of Psychiatry in Medicine, 37*(4), 371–381. https://pubmed.ncbi.nlm.nih.gov/17294840/

Texas Education Agency. (2024). *Employed teacher attrition and new hires 2014–15 through 2023–24.* Texas Education Agency, https://tea.texas.gov/reports-and-data/educator-data/employed-teacher-attrition-and-new-hires-2023-2024.pdf.

Vallée, D., & Fraser, S. L. (2022). Influence of flexible classroom seating on the well-being and mental health of upper elementary school students: A gender analysis. *Frontiers in Psychology, 13,* 918679. https://doi.org/10.3389/fpsyg.2022.918679

Vygotsky, L. S. (1978). *Mind in society: The development of higher psychological processes* (M. Cole, V. John-Steiner, S. Scribner, & E. Souberman, Eds. & Trans.). Harvard University Press.

Weston Public Schools. (2025). *Vision statement.* Retrieved March 16, 2025, from https://www.westonschools.org/district/vision-statement/

Will, M. (2022, May 31). Teachers are not okay, even though we need them to be. *Education Week*. https://www.edweek.org/teaching-learning/teachers-are-not-ok-even-though-we-need-them-to-be/2022/05

World Economic Forum. (2023). *The future of jobs report 2023*. World Economic Forum. https://www.weforum.org/publications/the-future-of-jobs-report-2023/

Ye, X. (2024). A review of classroom environment on student engagement in English as a foreign language learning. *Frontiers in Education, 9*. https://doi.org/10.3389/feduc.2024.1415829

INDEX

FSC
www.fsc.org
MIX
Papier | Fördert gute Waldnutzung
FSC® C083411

Zeitfracht Medien GmbH
Ferdinand-Jühlke-Straße 7
99095 Erfurt, Deutschland
produktsicherheit@kolibri360.de